Go Kiss the

Life Lessons
for the Young
Professional

World

SUBROTO BAGCHI

PORTFOLIO
PENGUIN

PORTFOLIO

Published by the Penguin Group

Penguin Books India Pvt. Ltd, 11 Community Centre, Panchsheel Park, New Delhi 110 017, India

Penguin Group (USA) Inc., 375 Hudson Street, New York, New York 10014, USA

Penguin Group (Canada), 90 Eglinton Avenue East, Suite 700, Toronto, Ontario, M4P 2Y3, Canada (a division of Pearson Penguin Canada Inc.)

Penguin Books Ltd, 80 Strand, London WC2R 0RL, England

Penguin Ireland, 25 St Stephen's Green, Dublin 2, Ireland (a division of Penguin Books Ltd)

Penguin Group (Australia), 250 Camberwell Road, Camberwell, Victoria 3124, Australia (a division of Pearson Australia Group Pty Ltd)

Penguin Group (NZ), 67 Apollo Drive, Rosedale, Auckland 0632, New Zealand (a division of Pearson New Zealand Ltd)

Penguin Group (South Africa) (Pty) Ltd, 24 Sturdee Avenue, Rosebank, Johannesburg 2196, South Africa

Penguin Books Ltd, Registered Offices: 80 Strand, London WC2R 0RL, England

First published in Portfolio by Penguin Books India 2008

Copyright © Subroto Bagchi 2008

18 17 16 15 14 13

ISBN 9780670082308

Typeset in Sabon Roman by SÜRYA, New Delhi
Printed at Chaman Offset Printers, New Delhi

GO KISS THE WORLD

For Susmita

Contents

# Acknowledgements

I will fail in my duty if I do not thank several individuals who have helped bring this book to you.

Writing a book is sometimes like sculpting with words. As you proceed, the sculpture that emerges is often different from what was in your mind. Worse, while trying your best, as it emerges, you do not quite know what the final form will look like—the sculptor experiences moments of profound pain during this process even as he chisels away. In moments like these, my editor, Sumitra Srinivasan, stood by my side and helped me with a sense of direction. I am grateful, Sumitra.

I am also grateful to my publisher, Ravi Singh, who took great personal interest and urged me to 'stay with the story'.

My brothers Debi Prasad and Amitav read the manuscript for accuracy of certain historical events, and colleagues Suma Thomas and Tridip Saha critiqued it during the early stages. Colleague Shanti Uday helped with version control, back-ups and other chores.

My cousin Pradeep Bagchi helped with valuable research.

Most importantly, I remain deeply indebted to the co-founder and executive chairman of MindTree, Ashok Soota, who gave me the space to write this book while I continue to serve the organization.

As with my earlier book, proceeds from *Go Kiss the World* will go to the MindTree Foundation that supports primary education, with special emphasis on children with disabilities.

Prologue

I was leaving for the United States, where I worked, after a two-week vigil by my mother's bedside in a hospital in Bhubaneswar, Orissa. She had suffered a near-fatal stroke. She was neither getting better, nor moving on. My wait was not helping. So I, her last born, thought it was time to get back to work.

On my way to the airport, I decided to stop by at the hospital one last time. An eerie midday quiet hung around the government hospital. Walking past listless cows and a couple of resident stray dogs in the compound, I entered her room. She lay on the bed, just like the night before, quiet and unmoving. I held her hand in my palms. After a few minutes, as I bent to kiss her forehead, wrinkled with age but still beautiful, she asked me in a garbled voice, '*Chumu kyano khaccho?*' Why are you kissing me?

'*Khabona kyano?*' Why not? I asked.

She replied, simply, '*Jao, jagat ta ke chumu khao.*' Go, kiss the world.

These were my blind mother's last words to me and they became the guiding principle of my life.

¤

The night-long vigil of the lone kerosene lantern in the room had blackened the top of its glass with soot. Around its flicker, Makhan Gopal Bagchi and his four sons—the eldest fourteen, followed by a thirteen-, twelve- and three-year-old—sat huddled under the tiled roof of the small government quarter they lived in. From the adjoining room came the sounds of groaning. Labonya Prova Bagchi had cooked, cleaned and kept house for her husband and four sons till this day, when she had gone into labour. Outside the house, beyond the community well that served the needs of the few families in adjoining government quarters and the undertrials of the nearby police lock-up, it was still dark.

Patnagarh, a small subdivisional town of five thousand people, seasonally cut off from the world by a river without an all-weather bridge, did not have a hospital. For the non-gazetted tehsildar, who was now expecting his fifth child, anxiety was mounting. While it was commonplace for childbirth at home in places like Patnagarh, he was not sure his wife would make it through this one without medical help. The family's only hope in case of an emergency was Dr S.K. Mitra and his wife, Manorama, an erstwhile lady health visitor. The couple lived half a kilometre away. He was not sure whether to send one of his sons to wake them up. He should wait some more, he thought, before disturbing the doctor. But with the groans becoming unbearable, he finally made up his mind.

'Go, call Mittir meshomoshaye,' he told the eldest boy.

After the Second World War, certain categories of medical professionals had been retrained so that they could become practising doctors. Armed with a medical licence, Captain S.K. Mitra had come all the way from the war to settle in Patnagarh, then under the rule of the king of Bolangir. Here he had met Manorama, a Christian lady from Maharashtra, who had come there to work as the only lady health visitor. The two had fallen in love, married and settled down to serve the small community. She was the only woman who could speak English; it had earned her the name 'memsaheb mashima' among the four boys. The Mitras weren't just doctors, they were like family. In the small town that was Patnagarh, everyone was kin to everyone else. The Mitras made little money, would charge nothing for emergencies like these and were always at hand.

The boy ran through the darkness. Mittir meshomoshaye's house seemed really far. Finally, he reached and after a breathless conversation, the doctor accompanied the young boy. The doctor's arrival meant some relief. While all one could do was wait, there was now hope that it would all end well. But even as Dr Mitra tended to Labonya, the moaning did not decrease. After some time, Dr Mitra opened the door and asked that his wife be called; it wasn't possible for him to handle the situation by himself.

Again the boy ran; this time dawn was breaking, the night sky softly illuminated. He had just passed his matriculation examination from the local Romai High School, named after an erstwhile king of Bolangir, with a first class—he had become the second student to get a first class from the vernacular school. With school over, he was waiting to go to Ravenshaw College in faraway Cuttack in a few days' time. The journey to Cuttack would mean a forty-kilometre, three-hour bus ride that would take him to Sambalpur. Then, an overnight bus to the sleepy railhead of Meramandali awaited him. There, the Talcher Passenger came once a day to take people all the way to Cuttack. The entire journey would take him nearly twenty-four hours. But right now, memsaheb mashima's house seemed further than that. He ran as fast as he could, and after what seemed an eternity, was finally banging on her door.

Memsaheb mashima rushed, half-walking, half-running. Just as she stepped on to the veranda, the groaning abruptly stopped and the full-throated cries of a newborn burst through the house.

My mother always told me I was born just when the big red sun emerged in the east and burst forth into a new day. I love this sheer imagery every time the story of my birth crosses my mind.

¤

My earliest memory of my childhood is when I was a three-year-old. From then, till today, I have watched myself grow up with the keenness of a photographer. Life becomes fascinating if we observe it even as we are living it. As I trawl through the archives of my life, I find an interesting path emerging. It curves twice—once in the beginning of my twenties; the other when I enter my forties. As I look around and see the lives of countless young professionals—doctors, engineers, policemen, teachers—I find the same sharp curves, each life divided into three distinct phases.

In Part I of the book, you will live and, hopefully, love my early years. You will see how character and values get imprinted in a child's mind; how displacement creates self-confidence and what a magical difference mentoring can make at any stage of our lives; experience the joy that is childhood, a wonderful gift that need never be left behind. I treasure my childhood, for if I forget it, the child in me will die.

In Part II, you will explore the making of a young professional who, like everyone else, wanted to 'be someone'. It is a familiar phase with its many ups and downs during which we realize the dissonance between the romance of youth and the reality of the workplace, though with some perspective and a certain mindset they can be aligned. I started my working life as a clerk in a government office and finally ended up co-founding MindTree—India's first venture-funded IT services company to get publicly listed.

At the source of a river, we have no idea of the path it will take to reach its confluence. Yet, I meet countless young professionals anxious about picking the right job and the right company, overplanning their careers. Their usual refrain is: How will this job help me in my career? But who on earth truly knows? In their anxiety to carve the perfect path, chanting 'What will I be, what will I be?', they overlook the importance of the smallest of jobs and forget that in our early lives, the job in itself is immaterial. What is material is the work ethic we build. Your first, the second, and even perhaps the third job will not build or define your career; the respect, patience, affection and gratitude with which you treat them will.

In Part III, I take you on the journey of my forties, even as it continues to unfold, to show you how I fell and got up, and how I learnt from people who have been there before me. For a successful professional, the decade of the forties becomes a defining period. It is a time that can almost be compared to assault camp, where preparations are made before climbing the final peak. It is alluring, and ruthless in its ability to weed out most contenders while pushing up the chosen one. This seldom happens in slow motion. Before you realize it, the outcome is staring you in the face. There is little one can do to rewind and reconsider choices, something life allows you when you are in your twenties. In this phase of life's journey, unless one handles oneself with contemplation and care, the precipice and not the pinnacle becomes the destination. I have seen countless overachievers who come up to this point and then must leave the professional journey of their choice.

Before you read on, I have two more things to tell you. The nature of the narrative requires that I constantly speak to you in the first person. Yet, my life has not been only about 'me, myself and I'. Without people around me, without their affection and warmth, I would not last even for a day. So, while my narrative requires me to use a lot of the 'I', you must discount its character, focussing instead on the journey and its lessons. Second, I have been candid and forthcoming about my life experiences— the only exception being my relationship with my wife Susmita. She grew up with me and has been an abiding influence on my professional career. Seldom can one reach the top without enlisting the support of a loved one. I cannot imagine where I would be today if she hadn't been by my side since she was fifteen. Ever since, she has remained my Rock of Gibraltar. However, to honour her wishes, I have kept our personal relationship outside the purview of this book.

Your life is a beautiful gift, unique to yourself. There is no other person in this universe quite like you. Which is why my life story in itself is not important; the important thing is what you take away from it. Even as you find some of my lessons interesting or useful, what really matters is how they lead you to your own reflection and your own life lessons. Nothing works better than that. And more than just living your life, the capacity to behold it is even more beautiful.

PART I

CHAPTER 1

Displacement and Progress

I was born in Patnagarh, Orissa in May 1957 four months before Sputnik, the first man-made satellite to orbit the Earth, was sent up, leading the great communication theorist Marshall McLuhan to foresee the collapse of time and space. He went on to coin the term 'global village', signifying the impact satellite technology would have in the decades ahead. Though not yet global in any sense, Patnagarh remains somewhere between a village and a town with a population of eighteen thousand in twenty-first-century India. Quite honestly, I have no real recollection of the place.

On arrival, memsaheb mashima had boiled some water, sterilized a new razor blade, taken some gauze and separated me from my mother, thereby putting me into my own orbit. In the days to follow, Dandorma, or 'Dando's mother', our domestic help, herself an untouchable, rubbed me vigorously, twice a day, with hot mustard oil to make sure I stayed there.

From Patnagarh, we moved to as many places as my father's junior-level state government job took him. For the most part, I grew up in tribal districts like Koraput and Keonjhar. The earliest recollection I have is of three places in Koraput district where I lived between the ages of three and eight—Rayagada, Nabarangapur and Koraput; the former two have since become full-fledged districts. The memory of each place is of a government house with no running water or electricity. But that did not mean hardship of any kind. It was a happy childhood marked by curiosity, contentment and a sense of progressive unfolding that, looking back, seems almost magical. By the time I was beginning to become aware of the world around me, the three older children were gone from home. So, barring their occasional visits, my childhood was just four of us—my mother, father, Aurobinda, the fourth son, and I.

The Rayagada house had a high veranda. Its cement surface was huge and served as a drawing board. The monthly grocery included boxes of chalk that were not rationed. This was a childhood set in India of the late 1950s when almost everything valuable—rice and wheat and sugar and kerosene—was rationed by the government and, in turn, by the mother in every middle-class household. All day long my brother and I drew pictures, often those of the idling steam engine across the railway tracks. Since there was no water at home, I used to be escorted to a municipal tap nearby where we bathed every day. I was a chubby baby and I remember the attention I got from the women who would come to fetch water for their homes and stood chatting near the tap that smartly gushed out mountain water at designated times. On one occasion, a young lady tried to hold me in her arms and that, for some reason, made me angry. I slipped out, took some mud in my tiny hands and threw it at her, soiling her sari. In my mind's eye, I can still see her astonished face. Even today that memory makes my heart break and if only I could see her one more time, I would buy her flowers and make amends. The other image of Rayagada, clear in my mind, is the sight of tractors dragging trailers laden with sugarcane to the only sugar mill the district was proud to have, and urchins running after them to drag the cane stalks at the end of the trailer. On occasion, when not being watched, my brother and I joined the great sugarcane desperadoes.

After Rayagada, we lived in Nabarangapur. Literally 'the place of the nine *ranga*s', or colours, it evokes memories of a dusty road to nowhere, upon which every evening a drunken old man would come tottering, abusing the government for its policy of prohibition. He would loudly proclaim that he would continue drinking and affirmed, '*Mu peeibee, ahuri mada peeibee. Gandhi budha kahichi, tu pee, ahuri mada pee.*' (I shall drink, and I shall drink some more. Old man Gandhi has told me to drink and drink some more.) The Paraja, the Kondha, the Bhumiya and the Domb—all indigenous people of

13

the place who had known no government and lived in peace and harmony since the beginning of time—were suddenly being told that they could not make liquor out of the rice they had cultivated, nor could they drink it. As civilization collided with freedom, the old man created the earliest image of resistance in my four-year-old mind.

From Rayagada to Nabarangapur to Koraput town, it was a fascinating journey. As a child, Koraput evoked a sense of timelessness for me. The picture of the outside world was one of beautiful forests, groups of peaceful Paraja tribal folk coming down from the mountains with forest produce to sell or to barter—firewood, some eggs, wild berries, tiny wild mushrooms that grew on top of anthills, bamboo shoots and occasionally a rooster. They sold these at the Sunday *haat*, an open-air market, purchased rice, salt, kerosene and liquor and went back to where they had come from. The Paraja womenfolk were colourfully dressed, their skin glistening with the purity of the rain forest, their bodies tattooed to enhance their appeal and to protect them from evil. The children were almost always naked; with happy faces and protruding bellies, they hung on to their mothers with shy curiosity. Occasionally, a well-fed family dog came along with vigilant eyes and a mountain pride that canines of the forest possess. In the evenings, one saw them return to their homes in the forest, mostly inebriated, singing and dancing in groups, the men and the women teasing each other through the lilting music.

The house we had in Koraput, in the foothills, was surrounded by big black rocks, wild mango trees, bamboo bushes, wild rose and other vegetation which grew in abundance. We spent half our time atop the trees and after every rain built dams across tiny rivulets that formed as easily as they vanished. When at home, I often spent hours following ants to find out where they ultimately went and their eternal busyness remains a fascination for me even today. In places like Koraput, there were no parks or designed play areas, no library and certainly no movie theatre. Some days, the sighting of a government jeep towards evening, carrying a portable projector and a cinema screen, used to bring electrifying excitement among the children of the neighbourhood. They would run to their homes to inform others and return with sacks and old bedsheets and whatever else they could find to reserve their favourite spot on the ground even as the jeep-folk set up the movie projector. It was all part of the efforts of the government's public relations department to let the people of Koraput know that there was a bigger world out there. The public relations people would first show 'news reels' through which the government dished out mild propaganda, followed usually by a feature film with a patriotic, reformist or moral overtone. Those who came in late and could not get a seat up front, chose to sit behind the screen, preferring to see the movie in reverse but at close quarters. Story had it that the first time the government brought this moving fare to the Paraja tribals up in the mountains hoping to befriend them, the tribal folk ran for their lives the moment the movie started, fearing that ghosts had been brought in by the government; as they ran, they pelted stones at their benefactor.

This was my idyllic life until 1964, when I turned seven. That is when the marching orders came. My eldest brother, Debi Prasad, whom we used to call Dadamoni, after his master's in economics had secured a teaching assignment at the university in Vani Vihar (literally 'the abode of the Goddess of Learning'). Simultaneously, he was going to prepare for the civil services examination. My father's dream was that Dadamoni join the coveted Indian Administrative Service (IAS). So, mother was to go and look after him for a year or so and, as her appendage, I was to go as well. Aurobinda was going to stay back with my father and continue schooling in Koraput. He went to the government-run district high school where he was in Class 6. I did not attend school because there were no primary schools nearby; I was being home-schooled.

I was excited about the proposed arrangement because, more than anything else, it meant a train ride to Bhubaneswar and going to the big city. After all, it was the capital of the state! Bhubaneswar even had two public buses that ferried people from one place to another within the town. That itself seemed so metropolitan!

The day finally arrived. Mother and I sat on a bus and then on a train to finally reach Bhubaneswar. I was wonderstruck—the well-laid-out roads, houses that had electricity, the huge overhead water tank that served the entire university population, the imposing library building, countless little shops selling sweets and condiments and coloured aerated cold drinks in bottles—it was a fascinating new world. Imagine a little boy who had never seen coloured, sweetened, aerated water that came in a bottle!

The move to Bhubaneswar was good for me. A few days after moving there, I was taken to the primary school on the university campus where, after a cursory interview, I was deemed fit to begin formal education and asked to report to the teacher in Class 5. It was my first taste of schooling. Soon, life settled into a nice routine for everyone. I went to school every day, Dadamoni went to the university and mother made sure that he got the nutrition that was required for an IAS aspirant.

After a year, when Dadamoni had made it into the IAS and mother's job was over, it was time to move again. We moved to Balasore, a district bordering West Bengal, where my father had been transferred. I joined a new school. My father's job in Koraput had been that of the district employment officer. He was sent again as the district employment officer to Balasore. More than my new school, Balasore itself was exciting. It was very different from Koraput or Bhubaneswar. The coastal border district was green, dotted with ponds and big jamun and other tropical trees laden with fruit. We had been there for only a few months when transfer orders came again. This time, father had been posted to Keonjhar as a 'leave reserve officer' with the revenue department. A leave reserve officer provided cover for people going on long leave and there was no predicting what kind of work would fall in his lap.

I clearly remember the jeep ride. In front, the driver, with father in the middle and mother on the far side. We two brothers were in the back, each commanding a side seat that had unrestricted view of a road that seemed to come from the front, far from the distant horizon, rushing back all the way; one could not tell if it was the road moving beneath us or the jeep moving on top of the tarmac.

Keonjhar, an erstwhile princely state, was home to ancient tribes like the Bathudi, the Bhuiyan, the Gond, the Ho, the Juang, the Kolha, the Munda and the Santhal. One of the world's most ancient rocks, thirty-eight thousand million years old, lies over a hundred square kilometres in Asanpat; there are frescos dating back to the fifth century AD in the caves at Sitabinj.

Locally the place is known as Kendujhar. Kendu is the name of a wild fruit tree whose leaf is used for holding the tobacco in beedis. *Jhar* means a stream that flows out of the earth. The place is probably named after a stream that presumably had its source under a kendu tree. The district headquarter was called Keonjhar Garh, the Fort of Keonjhar. I saw no fort there. There had been a king somewhere in the shadows of the past. More real was a huge building that was the district high school, appropriately named Dhanurjaya Narayan High School after the last noble to rule here.

I spent four years at Dhanurjaya Narayan High School but within that span we shifted house four times between my father's retirement and our moving into Dadamoni's house when he came to Keonjhar as a probationary IAS officer. Mercifully, just as father retired from government service, Dadamoni was posted to Keonjhar as subdivisional officer. When I completed Class 9, we moved again because Dadamoni was transferred to Chatrapur, a coastal district headquarter in the southern part of the state. I went along, studied there for a year and decided not to like the school. It was also in Chatrapur that my childhood affliction with bronchitis became full-blown asthma; occasionally I required hospitalization. On the one hand, I did not like my school and on the other hand, my health was clearly getting affected by the high humidity. The family agreed that I could go back to my old school at Keonjhar, all by myself, to complete my last year of high school. After a year there, I went to Bhubaneswar and joined BJB College where I earned a degree in political science over the next four years, before eventually beginning my work life.

¤

The fact that I changed five schools over eight years has developed in me a certain bond with displacement. Actually, it ran in the family. My grandfather had moved from West Bengal to Bihar. My father, in turn, went to Orissa in search of work. When my turn came, after my graduation, I eventually went to work in Delhi, then Calcutta, from there to Bangalore, to San Jose, California, back to Bangalore, then to New Jersey and back again to Bangalore. By 2008, I had been married for twenty-eight years and my wife Susmita and I had moved fourteen houses.

My life has not been merely about physical displacement; I have also constantly yearned to operate outside my comfort zone. I am not a management graduate, I did not study engineering, yet I have spent most of my life in the information technology (IT) industry, worked in the private sector, handled international assignments, and eventually co-founded a business that went all the way from 'idea to IPO'.

It is not necessary that everyone has wanderlust in their soul like me.

But it is important to know that quite often displacement is the key to progress, and we need to develop comfort with it. My early life experiences helped me build a high degree of comfort with displacement. Water in a pool is stagnant; only when it flows is it energized. The entire universe is in constant motion; even a moment of motionlessness is inconceivable in the cosmic state of things. Many professionals shudder at the thought of physical displacement, yet crave rapid mobility and growth in their careers.

When you are continuously displaced, you make friends easily. You have low expectations from the unfamiliar; hence you are more pleasantly surprised than frustrated when faced with life's many ups and downs.

You explore everything around you, develop curiosity—new lands, customs, food, and ways of doing things begin to draw you in.

You learn to survive on the strength of who you are, just for this day, today.

You build ingenuity in order to survive.

You trust strangers and, hence, strangers trust you.

You build intuitive capability to sniff trouble—which can tell you when to leave a bar!

You become an interesting person, because you have lots of stories to tell.

Finally, you learn to move on.

CHAPTER 2

Of Adversity and Faith

My mother was born the fourth child in a brood of six boys and girls. Her father was a lawyer in Pabna, now in Bangladesh. My third brother Amitav often teased her about whether grandfather was really a lawyer or just a *mukhtiar*, a para-legal. She would refuse to be dragged into the affectionately irreverent conversation, maintaining steadfastly that he was indeed a lawyer. We have no way of knowing.

When she was born in 1916, my grandmother, Prafulla Debi, nicknamed her 'Anna Kali'—a shortened form of '*Ar na Kali*' thereby inferring 'No more girls, please god'. In Hindu culture, just as the male child is seen as a form of Krishna, the girl child is equated to the many forms of the Mother Goddess, one of them being

Kali. Despite her devastating iconic imagery in most minds, in Bengal Kali is seen as quite benign and even loving. Since my grandmother had enough children, in my mother's name she encapsulated her prayer that she should please be spared more girls.

When mother was a four-year-old, one day a horse-drawn carriage stopped in front of the house and a few people brought down her father who had collapsed at the courthouse. He was suffering from meningitis; in a matter of a few days he died, leaving behind relatives who took away his property. His widow had to shave her head to bring to the notice of the entire world that she was dead for the purposes of the living. Her eldest son, barely out of his boyhood, yoked himself to pull the weight of a family of seven.

Widows in India, in those days in particular, had to shave their head, wear white clothes and abstain from all auspicious occasions, lest they bring bad luck. They had to give up non-vegetarian food; even onions and garlic were forbidden as they were said to stir earthly desires. Adhering to many serpentine rituals, widows were expected to just wither away. For Prafulla Debi, that wasn't an option. She had to raise her brood. In any Bengali family, fish is a part of the staple diet. As a mother of six, she had to cook fish for her children even though she had to stop eating it herself. One day, her mother came on a visit and was shocked at what seemed to be her widowed daughter's total incontinence. She screamed and demanded that my grandmother stop cooking fish forthwith. My grandmother pleaded that she had to feed six children and for their sake she could not stop handling fish. The grand old lady would have none of that, accusing her daughter of having become a *Khristan*, meaning a Christian, and threatened never to visit unless my grandmother vowed to live like a Brahmin widow. Prafulla Debi's response was that visiting her daughter was a choice the matriarch had to make; she had to do what was right for her children. My great-grandmother never visited her daughter again.

Grandmother eventually left Pabna and with her children came to a town called Berhampore in the district of Murshidabad in West Bengal. In Bengal of the 1930s it was not easy for women. Her eldest son had barely started working as a clerk to support the family. As the eldest male member, more out of a desire to protect his sisters than out of dogma, he insisted that they stop going to school. My grandmother threw a fit and insisted that the girls continue their education. Consequently, my mother went on to complete high school. She grew up on a heady diet of Bengali literature, music and patriotism. As a schoolgirl, she learnt to spin khadi as a symbol of self-reliance preached by Mahatma Gandhi. When the legendary Subhas Chandra Bose quit the Indian National Congress to advocate armed struggle against the British, she garlanded him. Her upbringing in a traditional Bengali, middle-class ethos was also characterized by spirituality and a certain mysticism. She was a beautiful woman; pretty outside and very strong inside.

When some people who knew both her and my

father's family brokered a proposal for matrimony, for the Moitras it was a match made in heaven. The Bagchis were relatively affluent, my father had a job with the king of Dhenkanal in Orissa, he spoke English like the British and was a very handsome man. The Moitras, in contrast, barely eked out a living—by the time my mother was of marriageable age, another brother had become a clerk and an elder sister had just started teaching. They still did not own a house and even though they never borrowed, they had nothing material to boast of. So, for them, the alliance was a blessing from the gods. On an auspicious day, my father arrived with a small contingent of relatives, married and took my mother to his parental house in Seraikella (in today's Jharkhand) and from there she came to Dhenkanal in Orissa. Transported to an alien land where she knew no one and did not speak the language, she came with the optimism that only a young bride is blessed with. Little did she know, it would soon be tested because her husband, perfect in every other way, periodically suffered from manic-depressive psychosis (MDP).

Mental illness afflicts at least one in every five persons in some form or other, transitionally or otherwise, in a country like India. It is mostly caused by genetic factors. Some of its many manifestations are depression, bipolarity, obsessive compulsive disorder, schizophrenia and so on. Most are manageable with clinical treatment, family support and the patient's will power. Many of the afflictions are caused by chemical imbalances that cause the brain to function abnormally; they are inherently physical disorders that are confused as mental illnesses and come with associated social stigma. In India, lack of awareness and education and even the absence of medically qualified doctors worsens the situation of such patients. Even today, there is only one psychiatrist per one million Indians. Back in the 1940s, the situation was grimmer.

By the time my mother realized her husband's illness, she had already given birth to three boys in quick succession—one in 1942, the second in 1944 and the third in 1946. No one had told her about my father's illness before she married him. Even today, in many families, people push these things under the carpet. In a 'don't ask, don't tell' world, young men and women, often with serious mental health issues, are married off in the hope that a marital relationship will solve all problems. For Labonya Prova, the door to the past was closed. With three sons, she could not go back to her brothers; they were ordinary people with little means. Her husband's family was sympathetic but everyone was busy with their own lives. Although my father's manic depression used to surface once in every ten years, it used to be severe enough for him to be taken to a mental asylum in Ranchi where he was given electric convulsive therapy. Each time he would return to resume his role as the breadwinner of the family.

A reticent man, he would become very assertive and garrulous during the episodes. He would try to do unusual things, forcing people to listen to what he had to say. There was an unfamiliar air of aggression about him during these times. With age, the frequency of the episodes increased.

I had no knowledge of my father's illness till I was eight years old; that was when he was hospitalized for the last time. Until then, I had never known him as anything other than an affectionate, doting man, who made it clear to me and to others around that I was his child prodigy, someone very special. My elder brothers though had known of it, and mother sent them telegrams to come and take him to hospital.

My mother called me aside and explained, 'Just as we all get physically unwell sometimes, people can get mentally unwell too. It is another medical condition. Your father will soon be perfectly all right. We have to send him for treatment. You have to give him time. Just make sure you do not bother him.' Somehow, things always worked out the way she said they would and after his treatment he came back the father I had always known.

I often wonder: Where would we all have been if my mother had not taken charge at this tipping point of her life when she realized her husband's medical problem for the first time? What would have happened if she had failed to come to terms with the situation and had caved in? Where would we be today if the family had gone into denial? Nearly six decades after, even today, it is amazing how pervasive that denial is in suffering individuals with unquiet minds and their families who prefer the shroud of secrecy to seeking expert help.

Labonya Prova was not a woman to either be helpless or blame others for her situation in life. I have never heard her recount her early life with my father with any despair. She gave him all the respect that was due to a husband and a provider. Though my father and my mother were temperamentally very different, they were bound by a very visible value system that glorified education, hard work, simplicity and honest living. She let him do his work in the service of the state as though he was next only to the Governor-General of India. His demands were non-existent—expect for a steady supply of good tea and a packet of cigarettes. Whatever mother cooked, he ate with contentment. He never touched alcohol, seldom socialized outside of work. He brought her a paltry sum of money at the end of the month and she took pride in the fact that the household never spent beyond its means. She moved with him from place to place, without complaint, often undertaking hazardous journeys, travelling through the night in remote areas.

As a magistrate in Dhenkanal district my father was required to tour the interiors, sometimes on a bicycle. He would be away for many days at a time. Those were the days without telephones, electricity and automobiles in most parts of India. Mother had to look after the house and manage the three older boys all by herself. One night, in Parjang, as she slept with her boys, a pack of bears descended and for hours they stood by the windows trying to break them. All she could do was hold her babies to her bosom and pray. More than once, it seemed that the windows would give way, but finally her prayers were heeded. The bears went away.

¤

Every time the family moved, the household effects fitted neatly into a trolley attached to a government jeep requisitioned for the purpose. As soon as we arrived at our destination, mother would send us to look for three bricks. While we were off getting the bricks, she would dig some fresh dirt and affectionately make mud out of it. When we brought back the bricks, she would build a *chulha*, an earthen stove, layering the bricks with the mud. In no time, three simple bricks and some mud would take the beautiful shape of a stove. She would then make some tea for everyone, thereby indicating the hearth of the home was set up, and that she was ready to cook and feed all of us. She took immense pride in her ability to build the nicest chulha that would last her until it was time to move again. She made friends with neighbours. She had no time for gossip, but was always at hand to help them. People came to take her advice, her curries were sent to other people's homes and their food came to ours.

In transferable government jobs, you can often be sent to places without knowing whether there is a good house, a good school or basic medical amenities in that place. When I see how much time government servants spend lobbying to land the right posting or move heaven and earth so they can stay away from a bad posting, my parents appear as aliens to me—they moved when told, no questions asked. When my father was posted to Athamallik, the only government quarter available was next to the morgue where dead bodies were brought in for post-mortem. Apart from the ghastly sight of a dead body arriving, often parts of the dissected anatomy would be strewn around after the post-mortem had been done. While digging the earth in her own courtyard to plant saplings, my mother would chance upon what looked like human bones. But what my mother dreaded most was the unbridled enthusiasm with which her three little boys would peer through the window whenever a corpse arrived. That scared her. Helpless, she would pray. Over time, something interesting started to happen. The day a corpse was to arrive for post-mortem, she would invariably see an apparition while saying her daily morning prayers. On cue, she would shut the boys inside the house. The same afternoon she would hear the familiar sounds signalling activity in the morgue. People build conviction in their god when confronted with miracles. She grew more steadfast in her faith with each adversity.

¤

When I was four or five years old, it became apparent to me that she could not see very well. She used to ask me to help her with threading the needle whenever she needed to mend an old garment. Her gradual loss of sight had started long before I was born. Apparently, she had developed early signs of a cataract. Once you develop cataract, you have to wait until it matures before it can be removed, and in those days it required an arduous surgery at a hospital in some big city with many weeks of post-operative care. My mother had to wait decades for her surgery, till the cataract matured in one eye and then, after many months, in the other eye.

As a result of her blurred vision, she could not read very well. She would ask me to read the daily newspaper to her. India was at war with Pakistan and she wanted to know every small detail of what was going on. As an eight-year-old, I was happy to read out loud stories of Indian tanks mowing down the enemy, our bombers breaking up supply lines by bombing out railway bridges and our fighters downing enemy planes. Eyes closed, she would listen, occasionally crying for the fallen and cheering for the brave soldiers of the nation.

When father retired from government service, Dadamoni took charge of the entire household. We acquired basic material comforts. For the first time in my life I had a wooden cot to sleep on, a table with two chairs were made for Aurobinda and me to study, a sofa arrived in the living room and my second brother, Shanti Swarup, brought home a transistor radio from the air force canteen. Amidst all this, mother received her eldest daughter-in-law. This was also the time when she was taken for her cataract operation all the way to the eye hospital Tata Steel ran in Jamshedpur. It was the longest I had stayed away from her. I did not mind the separation because soon she would be able to see. After weeks, she finally returned and, seeing me, exclaimed how fair I was! She had never seen me without the haze in her eye. Even today, I blush at the thought of her exclamation. It remains the biggest compliment any woman has ever given me.

When the cataract in her other eye matured, she was taken to an eye camp organized in a nearby mining township. Again I was left at home and prayed that she would return soon. When she did, she had to undergo weeks of post-operative care. During the cataract operation, the doctors had noticed a small mark in one of the eyes but did not think much of it, suggesting it may just be harmless. It was actually an ulcer, and it burst in her eye during the post-operative period. When the bandage was finally removed and my mother was asked to check her vision, she walked into a flower bed she and I had planted together—it had bloomed in riotous colour. It became clear to everyone that she was now blind in both eyes.

The first task for her was to learn to take care of herself. She learnt that slowly but surely, combing her own hair, bathing herself, changing clothes, then cleaning her own room and finally returning to the kitchen, this time only to cut the vegetables or knead the dough. When she knew that her blindness was irreversible, she stopped praying for herself. But she prayed more than ever before. For now, she had to pray for the whole world.

Many years later, when Susmita and I made our home, she came to live with us. My time with her used to be when I had my evening tea after work. She would listen intently to the day's events as Susmita and I talked. She had the power to comprehend a world so different from hers, a world separated by many walls including her loss of sight and only a high school education. But she could effortlessly scale those walls and I realize today that our ability to connect and comprehend is not so much a function of our education. Human potential is infinite and the fundamental requirement is not intellect but inclusion. She lived a life in which everything, just everything, belonged to her. She was life itself.

'The world is not divided between the living and the dead, there is no difference between what is animate and what is inanimate,' she once told me during our teatime conversations. '*Shabda* (sound) is *brhma* (life),' she added. Sensing that I was unable to comprehend, she knocked the surface of the dining table, twice, gently and asked, 'Where did the sound emanate from? Was it just my hand? No, it was the table replying to my knock. If I were to knock on any other surface, the sound will be very different, varied each time. It is the way the seemingly inanimate world speaks to you. There is brhma in everything. As long as you are willing to knock, even the inanimate will respond. Each time, without fail. Where there is shabda, there is brhma. Animate and inanimate are distinctions born of perception. In reality, everything is living.'

What did she experience with her two eyes that were open but had no vision in them? Did she only see darkness? 'No,' she had told me, 'I only see light, infinite light.'

Our vision is not always a function of our capability to see, it is our willingness to open up our inner eye to the limitless universe that lights up the path of our existence.

CHAPTER 3

Grace Under Pressure

My father was born to Dr Jogesh Chandra Bagchi and his wife Ganga Tarini Debi in 1910 in then undivided Bengal. Going by the patchy accounts of his growing up, his early life was probably divided between Seraikella, where my grandfather was employed by the local king, a village in West Bengal named Dhodadaha, where the family had vast tracts of ancestral land, and the city of Calcutta where my father was sent to study engineering, which he did not complete. My father was the second son in a family of nine surviving children. Four others had died very young.

Dr Jogesh Bagchi came to Seraikella by chance. After studying medicine at Calcutta Medical College, he seemed unable to get a job anywhere. In the beginning of the twentieth century, only a Britisher was accepted as a practising physician in most places. Abandoning his search for a job, he set up his own practice at Baithak Khana Road close to Sealdah Railway Station in Calcutta. Among his patients were the family members of the king of Seraikella and impressed with his capabilities, kept asking him to come to Seraikella. The doctor finally had to pay heed when one morning the king sent his personal salon car on the erstwhile Bengal Nagpur Railways (BNR) to fetch him. A smart move for talent acquisition even by today's standards!

After his first visit, he agreed to relocate to Seraikella on the condition the king set up an operating theatre that would have electricity, a thirty-bed hospital with a segregated women's ward and trained female nurses. My grandfather thought these conditions would deter the king. After several months, the king sent word—Dr Bagchi arrived at Seraikella to find that the king had actually set up the entire infrastructure, including a power generating plant, the first of its kind in the region, to provide uninterrupted electricity to the hospital. And this was how my grandfather settled in Seraikella, a sleepy little town, whose nearest recognizable geographic coordinate till date remains the steel city of Jamshedpur.

History never cared much for Seraikella. But, the British did. So, it was made a vassal state under the Empire. The king's subjects were largely local tribal folk—the Hos, the Santhals and the Kols. When my grandfather arrived there as a young man to look after the health of the king and his subjects, his job as civil surgeon included looking after the jail as required by British law. Even today, the civil surgeon of a district oversees the jail; it is not under the police. Apart from this, the king also ordained, '*Babu, saheb paar korte habe.*' My grandfather had to keep visiting Englishmen at bay. Unusual though the job requirement was, Dr Bagchi thought nothing of it and agreed. After all, he was the only one who could speak English in the whole of Seraikella, so it was indeed reasonable for the king to ask for such an expansive job description of the young doctor.

My grandfather, so far the only doctor the clan has ever produced, worked, lived and died in Seraikella. By the time my parents got married and came to the house the old doctor had lived in, he was no more. My grandmother had died even earlier. Yet, his legacy lived on.

My recollection of Seraikella is of a dusty little place with a bus stop, a police station, a small courthouse, a few grocery stores, a 'palace' that I never saw and a rivulet named Kharkai that wound through this place of obscurity. I have, on occasion, run away with a cousin to bathe in its waters. But all the aunts would tell us stories of how the river must swallow one man every year. As myth went, one year the river even swallowed the king's brother. Such stories of inherent danger made bathing in the river even more attractive—we developed a forbidden love for the river.

In 1975, as an eighteen-year-old, I visited Seraikella for a couple of days. On the day I was leaving, my uncle, a lawyer and the only son who had stayed on there to make a living, came to see me off at the bus station. In small towns, a bus station is a place for general congregation, a place where arrivals and departures, however insignificant, are a social event. As I was about to board the bus, a hoary old man, bent over his wooden staff came forward and asked my uncle who I was. My uncle said, '*Budha daktor-er nati eta.*' I was the grandson of the old doctor. After some rough calculation in his head, the old man refined his query: '*Eta Habur chha?*' He had recognized me correctly as 'Habu's child'. Habu was my father's nickname. Only in places where time moves slowly, people care so much about relationships.

Budha daktor had married off his two daughters when they were very young and sent his eldest son, Binode Gopal, to study medicine at Carmichael College in Calcutta. After completing his intermediate in science from Ravenshaw College, Cuttack, my father was sent to study engineering at Bengal Engineering College, Shibpur. Then one day, with the three younger boys still in school and the youngest a toddler, tne old doctor died. The king asked Binode Gopal and Makhan Gopal to return and take charge of their four younger siblings. Binode Gopal got a job with the state government and my father was sent to Dhenkanal with a letter of recommendation from the king of Seraikella. The king had given his daughter in marriage to the prince of Dhenkanal, an equally small vassal state in Orissa. Armed with the letter, my father came to the durbar of the king of Dhenkanal and was absorbed as assistant secretary of state for war affairs.

The world war which the British Crown was fighting never came to Dhenkanal. But, as a vassal state, war dispatches were received from London from time to time—the Queen liked to keep all her subjects informed of England's progress in the war. One of my father's responsibilities was to make sense of the dispatches and to keep the king in a state of virtual inclusion. My grandfather had taken great care to give his two older boys a good start in life, including private tuition by an Englishman whose fees were paid in gold coins. They had to master the English language so well that they could be considered on par with a 'London matriculate'. Long after, when my father was posted in remote areas where there were no schools, he personally taught us English. He would always tell us that his primary goal in life was to make us on par with London matriculates. Consequently, we never felt that we were missing out on life's opportunities by being raised in rural India, nor did we complain that we did not have the advantages of city life. After all, we could read, write and speak English like the English did.

Father was also charted with responsibilities of law and order and collection of revenues, and other occasional errands like escorting the entourage of the princess to Calcutta along with her dogs, Rex and Regina, where she delivered a baby boy. He used to travel many miles on a bicycle on his tours and eventually even had an elephant as his official vehicle. All in all, he must have done reasonably well for himself because he remained in the service of the king until one day such kingdoms were abolished and he became part of the Orissa state civil service.

During the amalgamation of Dhenkanal with Orissa state in 1948, an officer of the Indian Civil Service (ICS) who was entrusted with the task asked my father to return to Bihar. 'You are a Bihari, go back to Bihar,' he said. Makhan Gopal Bagchi refused to comply—this was his place of work, this was where he wanted to raise his children. The enraged ICS officer ordered his transfer to a smaller place and demoted him two levels. From being a first-class magistrate, he was relegated to a non-gazetted tehsildar with the powers of only a second-class judicial magistrate. In those days the executive and the judiciary were not separated and whether you were a first- or a second-class magistrate determined the categories of offences you could hear. Years later, Dadamoni was adjudged the best all-round student at Ravenshaw College in Cuttack. The prize for that distinction had been instituted by the family of the same ICS officer who had demoted my father and ruined his career.

My father never held any rancour against the officer who had demoted him because he had opted to stay on in Orissa for a larger goal: that of sending his children to college there. He had studied at Ravenshaw College and he was determined his sons too must graduate from the same college. The demotion that permanently damaged his seniority seemed a small price to pay, and with Dadamoni's accomplishment as the best student, all was quits now for my father.

Makhan Gopal Bagchi expected his children to grow up as upright, honest people who could hold their ground without fear or favour. He asked for tenacity ahead of ambition and required us to move on from the lows of life.

There are the inevitable times in every life when we all must step on a thorn. It is never a pleasurable feeling, it is not meant to be. In that moment of pain, more often than not, we are focussed not just on the pain itself but on the anguish of being singled out, asking the inevitable 'Why me?' question. In the larger scheme of things, that question is as irrelevant as the pain itself. All of us realize this sooner or later. What many of us do not comprehend, is the futility of carrying the baggage of that pain into our future. As I step on the thorn, if I begin to blame the thorn, the pain has a tendency to linger; sometimes the pain expands as time passes, its memory holding centre stage, colouring how we view and feel about our lives. In life, we cannot avoid pain. What we can do is learn from the pain and move on.

CHAPTER 4

The Power of Mentoring

'Dadamoni', in Bengali, literally means 'the gem among brothers'. I came under Dadamoni's tutelage when mother and I moved to Vani Vihar. The age gap of fourteen years between us made him part eldest brother and part father. While waiting to be admitted to the university's primary school on campus, I had nothing to do. I would, at times, sneak out of the house and wander around the university's corridors and classrooms. I found these to be fascinating places. The sight of young men and women walking around with fat books in their hands and hope in their eyes, the wise professors who often walked in twos and seemed so knowledgeable and happy and engaged in conversation, the beautiful library building—everything just pulled me in. Sometimes, I would even stand outside classrooms, eavesdropping on postgraduate lectures.

On one such occasion, I was peeping into a classroom where Dadamoni was teaching and he spotted me. I ran away. When he came home that evening, instead of punishing me, he asked me what I had been doing there. I sheepishly told him that I had been listening to him.

'What was I teaching?' he asked.

'You were telling them something about demand and supply,' I replied.

'What about it?'

'You were saying that with only one buyer and one seller, it is very difficult to fix the price of anything.'

He was impressed. He started explaining the theory of demand and supply to me in greater detail—how a marketplace worked, how prices were fixed and the co-relation of price with demand and supply. He took my curiosity seriously enough to periodically tell me about money and banking and finance. He taught me the law of marginal utility.

'Suppose you like to eat oranges, and keep eating one after the other, the first one will make you happy, the second one probably even happier still, you'll probably enjoy the third, but then a time will come when you will no longer be able to get that same satisfaction from every additional orange you eat, and if I keep insisting that you have more, it will probably make you feel sick. This is diminishing utility.' I nodded—it made perfect sense because I had felt sick after eating too many sweets just a few days earlier. In the days and months that followed, he told me about economists like Alfred Marshal and Adam Smith. With each lesson, I found myself elevated to a different level.

The annual university Chancellor's Cup debate competition was due—the best debaters from various colleges had come together to compete. Dadamoni asked me to come along to hear the competitors on the condition that I sit quietly at the back. I was mesmerized by the young men and women who came up to the podium to passionately debate the motion. I did not understand most of what they said, but the process was spellbinding. I told myself that, someday, I had to engage in this kind of thing.

On joining the IAS, Dadamoni was posted at Keonjhar where he was trained in various aspects of district administration, from overseeing land settlement in villages to declaring Section 144 in disturbed areas during a student strike. He always treated me like an adult, talking to me about the Indian Penal Code (IPC) and the Criminal Procedure Code (CrPC), the concept of segregation of power between the executive, the legislature and the judiciary, the working of grass-roots organizations like the panchayat system, the intricacies of the revenue administration and issues of development—it was as if I was his understudy.

Keonjhar has one of the world's richest deposits of iron ore and during the days of the cold war, India used a lot of mining equipment from east European countries. The ore was exported to various countries. When the Hungarian ambassador came on a visit to Daitary, an iron-ore mine, Dadamoni had to play host since Daitary was in his subdivision. He took me along to meet the ambassador. On the way from Keonjhar to Daitary, as I sat next to him in his official jeep, he explained the concept of official protocol—how an ambassador actually represented the sovereign—and coached me to address the ambassador as 'Your Excellency'. I couldn't wait for the visitor to ask me a question to show off that I knew how to address him correctly even though I was a small boy. I still remember the poor man's bewildered expression when I replied to his innocuous question, 'What is your name?' with 'Your Excellency, my name is Subroto Bagchi.'

In addition to the intricacies of district administration and diplomatic protocol, Dadamoni also taught me Rabindranath Tagore's timeless verse 'Where the Mind Is Without Fear'. It came in handy because I shifted schools every other year. The fact that I could recite an English poem by Tagore earned me instant acceptance in the eyes of my new teachers and my peers, who spoke little English themselves.

¤

Shanti Swarup was my second eldest brother. We lost him prematurely a few years before we lost mother. At home, he was called 'Winston' because my father loved Churchill. As soon as Winston completed his high school with flying colours, he was sent away to join the air force because my father could not afford the burden of simultaneously paying for the education of two sons in college and the resultant expenses for hostel accommodation. Places like Rayagada, Nabarangapur and Koraput in those days had no local colleges. That was a pity because Winston was the most brilliant among the five of us. He joined the air force as an airman. He came home on his annual holidays and it was a time for good food and a lot of joy because he brought small gifts for everyone. Among them, it was his duty to bring seeds of cosmos, petunia, zinnia and marigold for mother's garden every year.

Since he was in the armed forces, I always thought he killed enemy soldiers. I didn't know who the enemy was, and whenever I would bug him to tell me how many enemy soldiers he had killed, he would make up a new number each time—they varied widely beyond belief, but I was happy that he was at least killing some. Rather than engage me with war anecdotes, he would insist on teaching me how to polish shoes such that you could see your face in them. Even today, long after we have all grown up and Winston is no more, I still take pride in my ability to make a shoe shine.

We saw him only once a year ever since I can remember but every vacation he taught me something new. I remember how elated the family was when he finally got the rank of a junior commissioned officer—up from a sergeant. It meant a visible shift in status and attendant perks. Now he could travel, not by second class, but by first class while coming home by train for his annual vacation. As he got down at the railway station after his maiden first-class ride, he patted me on the head and said, 'If you want a guy to do a first-class job, give him a first-class ticket.' I nodded in boyish wonder but every time I look at organizations and their obsession with making life better for the folks at the top at the expense of the smaller folk who actually matter, I remember those words and the pride the entire family felt when one Winston got a first-class ticket. I am sure he also did a first-class job.

Though I have some fond memories of his visits, they are always accompanied by a sense of goodbye. As a result, he was always the visitor and lacked the relative permanence in my consciousness of either Dadamoni or Amitav.

¤

My third brother Amitav, a good eleven years older to me, studied at a college in a town near home. Because of this proximity, he visited home more often than Shanti Swarup. Amitav's nickname at home is Bulbul but a three-year-old me could somehow only pronounce it as Buldul, and I continued to call him that even as I grew up.

Dadamoni and Amitav grew up to be very different people, but both became role models for me in different ways. While Dadamoni excelled by treading the middle ground, Amitav lived on the edge, walking to a different drummer. A born rebel, he always questioned the system every step of the way and lived life on his own terms.

Amitav failed Class 5 because he did not like his teacher. He once ran away from home as a little boy. In college, he was thrown out for his anti-establishment activities and student activism. My father, a man of very little means, a man who hated politics and politicians, threatened to cut off financial support to him unless he quit politics. Amitav would not give in to that condition. To him, freedom to decide his own course was more important. He told my father that he would rather fend for himself. He was president of his college union and during his tenure he brought the entire state to a halt with a prolonged agitation, was shot at point-blank range by law enforcement officials, escaped by a miracle, and through all this remained unaffected by my father's rejections. The two agreed to disagree. His active involvement in politics took a rear seat when he had to choose a career and take up part of the family's financial burden. He joined the legal profession at the bar and following a period of initial struggle eventually started doing quite well. But then he wanted to get back to active politics. That did not quite work out for him. He took to alcohol that sent him to the brink and suddenly one day, he just quit alcohol, politics, his practice at the bar, his wife and two young sons and went away in search of god, wandering for a good twelve years as a man of religion, before partially returning to his family after his second son died in a tragic accident.

There is something fascinating about Amitav. He could have an engaging conversation on the future of humanity, world affairs, history and religion or any other topic. But more important was his ability to be one with ordinary people, his inclusive nature, to love and be loved. He lived for others before he lived for himself. As a student in the hostel, my mother would give him a blanket or a sweater every winter, and the next time he came home, rest assured, he would not have it, having given it away to some poor person. Rickshaw pullers, petty shopkeepers, students, teachers, bureaucrats, policemen and politicians would do anything for him. When he spoke at public meetings, he could electrify his audience. The poorest of the poor went to him with their problems; he was there for them through drought, flood or any other natural disaster. Wherever he went, people gave him food, shelter and anything else he needed.

He had ample opportunity to become materially very successful in life but every time something would make him opt out of the race for position and power. When he quit his law practice to become a hermit, everyone was worried what would happen to his family. He wondered what would have happened to them if he had been run over by a truck. Some were angry at what they saw as his irresponsibility towards his wife and children, some called him an escapist, some were simply dumbfounded by his decision and some thought he was a great soul in search of life's true meaning. None of these opinions mattered to him. He simply went away.

India doesn't let its hermits go hungry. For twelve long years, Amitav roamed from place to place. Sometimes he was seen in Puri, sometimes high up in the mountains in Kapilas and sometimes with a Vaishnavite sect. He survived.

Amitav returned to perform the last rites for his second son, who when reviving from a bad accident and a bout of jaundice at the same time, lost his balance, fell down and died in the prime of his youth. During his activist days, Amitav routinely used to take care of the last rites for any unclaimed dead body. And now he had to do so for his son.

We reached the burning ghat around midnight. There were half a dozen dead bodies in different stages of cremation, the mourners all gone. Cold rain was coming down; the wind played havoc with the fire. The body on the pyre would not burn, the smell of flesh and water and fire made standing there an ordeal. The men who make a living cremating the dead, moved from one corpse to another, bamboo stick in hand to turn the corpses. Having worked the whole day, they were too tired to fight the elements and started leaving.

Amitav did not leave. He stood by the pyre of his son, coaxing the body that had once played in his lap as a baby, to be one with the reluctant flames, turning it, pushing it, adjusting it with a bamboo stick gently, as if beseeching it to return to where it had come from. His face remained stoic behind the long matted hair and flowing beard; he did not cry.

¤

As my mentor, Dadamoni had a Pygmalion effect in shaping my personality and my destiny. Learning gives us knowledge but it is good mentoring that gives us the ability to relate it to the real world; it helps us learn life skills and moulds our attitude. The self-confidence that mentoring can generate is huge. The principles of mentoring a child and a budding professional are not different. It all begins with the magical sensation of someone reaching out and whispering into your ears, 'Yes, you can!' This is when dreams are created, and bridges built, to reach beyond the realm of the possible.

I learnt the importance of ambition and achievement from Dadamoni; from Amitav, I learnt that our achievements are only as good as the value they create for others. He also taught me that in the larger context of life and living, the line between what is mine and what isn't is just another porous continuum. In it, the gaps, the empty spaces that make the line porous, are the reality. These intermittently laid lines are just our perception, they are drawn by a mind that is not fully awake to the deeply interconnected nature of things. All professional growth must finally take us to that point of realization because quantum achievement follows a state of awareness in which the concept of mine and thine ceases to exist.

¤

I count my blessings for the early-life influences of my family on me.

In many ways, we are all surrounded by such people all the time—sometimes they are siblings, sometimes friends, teachers and co-workers. As we get on with the concrete busyness of life, we lose our capacity to receive from people.

The capacity to receive asks for humility. Humility makes the mind an empty vessel that then can receive.

The capacity to receive expands when there is the willingness to give back—only when we return what we receive, are we blessed to receive even more.

CHAPTER 5

Building Memorability

Looking back, my schooldays were filled with a sense of enchantment, of constantly exploring new possibilities.

My days at Keonjhar dominate my memories of school. I arrived at D.N. High School in the middle of the academic session for Class 6. It was a bewildering experience. The entire class sat on the floor on a dhurrie that had large holes in a few places and the teacher hovered over our tiny heads with a long, menacing stick broken from the abundantly growing *amari* bushes right behind the classroom. The roof was sky high, made with earthen tiles, under which sparrows hatched. It was commonplace for an occasional egg to drop on someone's head causing excitement and confusion. Often one could find a baby sparrow that had been evicted by the parents from their nest ending up in some boy's school bag. Since I arrived late in the academic year, the seating arrangement had already been finalized by the teacher. The smaller boys, who were usually the brighter ones, sat up in front. The last couple of rows were populated by the bigger boys who had invariably failed once or twice before. I ended up getting a seat with them. They taught me to catch harmless green grass snakes that we kept in our pockets to scare others. Sometimes, we sneaked out to see the lonely human skeleton kept in the science laboratory—it was the only object of awe the laboratory had, and only students of Class 8 and above could study him. When I did eventually make it to Class 8, I had lost interest in the poor guy. More interesting things engaged us by then.

Schooling was free, though every child had to pay two rupees a month for lunch, which was actually a snack. The so-called lunch arrived around midday in a bucket and as soon as its aroma invaded our nostrils, we would get wildly distracted. It was the most exciting thing about school—*mudi*, puffed rice mixed with savouries, two fried potato chops and maybe a sweet on special occasions like Independence Day or Republic Day.

Mother, father, Aurobinda and I lived with Dadamoni's family in a sprawling old bungalow meant for the subdivisional officer. Behind our bungalow was a village of untouchables. We did not entertain the notion of untouchability at home and I had a few friends from school who lived there. I used to go to their house and spend long hours playing with them. One day, word arrived that all the villagers had gone to chase a bear that had come down from the mountains. Without informing anyone at home, I scampered away to join them. After running through miles of green paddy fields that separated the village from the mountains, I found the villagers. The bear chase was unlike anything I had ever seen. Hundreds of stick-, sickle- and spear-wielding men and boys ran after the full-grown bear. The bear appeared confused more than anything else, running helter-skelter. When the bear turned to face the villagers, they would start running in the opposite direction. Then the bear would turn course and run in the reverse direction, with the villagers following him. After this had gone on for a while, the bear just collapsed in exhaustion and all the villagers swooped down on him. The poor bear was killed and everyone started pulling out his hair because the villagers believed that a strand of bear hair tied around a patient's neck could bring down high fever. I brought home some bear hair too with the expectation that I would be given a hero's welcome. Instead, a good thrashing awaited me for having run away in the middle of homework and gone missing for a couple of hours. The bear hair brought no relief from the heat at home and I realized it hadn't been such a good idea after all.

Leaving aside the bear chase, I generally engaged in constructive pursuits. I was part of the school gymnastics team and being a tiny fellow, got the chance to be right on top of the human pyramid, the one who saluted on behalf of the formation. At home, I extracted an agreement from my mother that if she would fund a small poultry, I would supply her with the eggs the family needed in exchange. Off I went to the haat and returned with a rooster and a bunch of hens. I also worked hard and did quite well at school and joined every debate and essay competition. When I was in Class 8, I enrolled in the National Cadet Corps (NCC). This became a serious passion in later years and I continued with it in college.

When it was time for me to choose either humanities or science for further studies, I chose to study the former simply because Aurobinda had done so. Looking back, it was an uninformed decision and if I were to make the choice again, I would probably have chosen science so that I could study medicine. I think I would have made a good doctor.

¤

After high school, my search for a college brought me to Bhubaneswar. I enrolled in a degree course in political science at BJB College. It wasn't very difficult to make the choice because Dadamoni was now posted in Bhubaneswar and I could stay with his family. Looking back, the years between 1972 and 1976 are the golden period of my adolescent life. The rustic days of Keonjhar were over. I was back in the state capital. At college, I liked my teachers a lot, the academic environment was very good and the newness of the subjects I was learning kept me engaged. My early childhood fascination for debating as a hobby came full circle when I won the Chancellor's Cup. As an NCC cadet, I was selected to train for two months at the Air Force Para Training School at Agra where I earned 'Para Wings' as a qualified paratrooper after jumping out five times from a Child Packet aircraft of world war vintage. My paratroop regimen with the air force cured my lungs of the bronchial asthma that had hospitalized me before and brought me new hope.

In January 1975, I was selected as part of the state NCC contingent for the Republic Day parade in New Delhi. It was an exciting opportunity for me, a chance to visit the country's capital. Equally exciting was that this gave me the chance to compete to be selected as the best cadet of India. Each participating state nominated its best cadet and all the best cadets competed with each other for the national honour. The fact that it was a contest among the best made it obvious that each cadet was as good as the other when it came to the basic skills of drill, discipline and turnout. The final choice was really made based on two rounds of interviews—first with a panel of senior defence officers, after which only four shortlisted cadets were presented before the director general of the NCC. He chose the best cadet of the year. The honours that followed included receiving the trophy from the prime minister, and a ceremonial breakfast at the prime minister's official residence where the best cadet received a sandalwood cane of honour. Then, there was a formal introduction to the President of India at

Rashtrapati Bhavan. All in all, the stuff dreams are made of.

Following tradition, no best cadet of any state is told that he is a nominee till an hour before the all-contestants' line-up. All you knew was that you had contested at the state level before coming to Delhi. So, when an officer came and told me to don my uniform and report for the selection panel in fifteen minutes, I was both pleased and anxious. After the contestants had gone through the basic drills, they were called into a tent where a three-member selection team sat. These were officers who had prior experience recruiting for the armed forces. The interview was similar to that for aspirants to the Indian Military Academy. When my turn came, I marched into the tent, saluted and took my seat. The chairman of the panel, a colonel in the army, shot the first question: What did I know about Diego Garcia?

It was 1975, four years after the Indian Army had gone into the then East Pakistan to help the Mukti Bahini rebels who were fighting the Pakistani Army to give birth to Bangladesh. Following large-scale refugee exodus into India, the Indian Army had to be sent to resolve a humanitarian crisis of gigantic proportions. The United States, as an ally of Pakistan, had moved its famous Seventh Fleet into the Indian Ocean to checkmate India. Around that time, in another act of balance of power, the United States substantially increased its presence in the Indian Ocean on an island named Diego Garcia with rapid deployment strike capability in the region. It was a continuing sore point in the Indo–US bilateral relationship.

I realized the panel was checking my knowledge of current affairs. I told the panel all I knew about Diego Garcia—the history of the largest island in the Chagos Archipelago that was transferred by the British to the Americans; about its strategic military importance; the exact distance of the island from Kanyakumari, the southernmost tip of India; the length of the runway and about its proposed extension to twelve thousand feet; the number of B-52 bombers stationed there and how long it would take a long-range B-52 bomber from Diego Garcia to reach New Delhi and return without refuelling.

The panel did not ask me any further questions. My years of reading the front page of the newspaper first and then reading the editorial out loud to father every morning as a child had paid off. I got shortlisted as one of four cadets to be interviewed by the director general the next day. He had to choose the best of the best on the basis of an unstructured meeting with all four cadets at the same time. The meeting with the director general was easy but left me wondering about the outcome. There was no knowing who the chosen one would be. Finally, the day before the Republic Day parade I received the news that I had been chosen as the best NCC cadet of the country.

My purpose in recounting this story is not to talk about my achievement. It is to emphasize the importance of creating memorability in your first meeting with anyone. Most people we meet do not have a special reason to remember us, nor are they interested in what we have to say or what we actually do. We live in a world of information overload and attention deficiency. People we meet are often looking at us but thinking about something else. Given that, it is important that in every situation one has to be not only well prepared but razor-sharp to create instant engagement. Be it a job interview, a presentation, or a meeting, we all have a very short window to make the right impression, and unfortunately most of us miss it. The question on Diego Garcia had given me that short window to make my mark. It is what I call the Diego Garcia moment of my life.

CHAPTER 6

The Future of Desire and the Future of Fate

When I returned to Bhubaneswar after the Republic Day parade, I was a minor celebrity. More awards and recognitions followed—the chief minister of the state honoured me at the subsequent Independence Day parade, the governor invited me home. It gave me a certain cocky confidence that only an eighteen-year-old is entitled to. For a while, the whole world looked like it was my play field. There is something about being young and achieving some success that makes you think you are invincible.

For me, that was soon to change.

¤

J.D. Bernal wrote in *The World, the Flesh and the Devil* way back in 1929 that 'There are two futures, the future of desire and the future of fate, and man's reason has never learnt to separate them.' I have always intimately felt the power of these words.

For the most part, I had grown up under Dadamoni's care. In those days, middle-class families prided themselves in their ability to produce civil servants. The best students were meant to serve the republic just as, prior to independence, they were meant to join the ICS under the British Crown. If not the civil services, they joined the military. As the best NCC cadet, I could have walked into the armed forces. There is something about uniformed jobs that fascinates me even today. But somehow, deep inside, I knew there wasn't enough of a pull and by the time I graduated from college, I had pretty much ruled it out as a career option.

During the later years in college, I somehow developed a fascination for academic research and the study of international relations. Jawaharlal Nehru University (JNU) in New Delhi offered a postgraduate programme in international relations and I felt pursuing that could give me freedom from Bhubaneswar. I needed a different orbit, as we all do from time to time. Enrolling in JNU would help keep my options open—either becoming a teacher or succumbing to the traditional mould of the civil services.

In the two months after I graduated, everything changed forever. It became clear to me that financing the two-year residential programme at JNU would not work out despite the national scholarship I was entitled to. Those days, a national scholarship was a grant of one thousand two hundred rupees a year, but it was disbursed in two half-yearly instalments. It could probably pay for half the cost of education in JNU. The real issue was cash flow. Banks did not provide educational loans for studying humanities, and I did not want to remain a burden on the family. The really affordable option was for me to stay on in Bhubaneswar. Dadamoni was in the IAS no doubt, but he had borne the family burden far too long and I did not want him to continue to finance my education. Shanti Swarup was now a junior commissioned officer in the air force and he had his own family to look after. Father's pension was meagre. Amitav, who was restarting life as a lawyer, did not have a steady source of income. He had willingly taken up the responsibility of looking after us because Dadamoni was now posted away from Bhubaneswar. Aurobinda, who had graduated with me, had decided to join the Indian Army and was soon going to take care of himself.

After some deep thinking, I reconciled to joining Utkal University in Bhubaneswar and enrolled for a postgraduate degree in political science. I attended class for exactly two months. Neither the curriculum nor the faculty excited me. The courses seemed a repetition of what I had already learnt in my graduation. The thought of marking time for two long years till I was old enough to sit for the IAS examinations, the socially acceptable thing to do, was dreadful. Every day became a drag. At nineteen, I felt I was at a crossroads. There had to be a way out, I told myself.

I became seized with the idea of looking for work. Those days the government was the only employer in Orissa. Industry was next to non-existent; the private sector simply did not exist. I decided to meet my friend Priyadarshi Mahapatra's father, Narendra Mahapatra, who was a deputy secretary in the local secretariat. He was in the industries department and I felt talking to him could provide me with some leads. He gave me a patient hearing and told me that the only jobs that would open up soon were those of lower division clerks. If I was really keen, I could show up for a test the next day. The positions were temporary, paid three hundred and five rupees per month and would allow me to attend law classes in the evening. The next day I gave the written test, was later called for an interview and qualified to become a lower division clerk with the small industries section of the industries department of the Government of Orissa. In the great administrative pyramid, only the peon, who served tea and moved files from one table to another, would be junior to me in rank. But I did not care. Three hundred rupees was the rent we paid for the house in which my parents, Amitav, his wife, Aurobinda and I used to live. So, it was good enough. It was better than wasting time at the university.

¤

The secretariat building, which houses the ministers and the bureaucracy, is the most imposing structure in Bhubaneswar. The less conspicuous legislative assembly building is adjacent but separate. Another potential contender, the red brick high court, built during British rule, remains in the twin city of Cuttack. With no other significant architectural competition, the white secretariat building, with its sprawling gardens, imposing high gates with a sentry, and the tricolour proudly fluttering on top provided tangible evidence that the state was not withering away any time soon. There, I started my professional life as a lower division clerk on 1 November 1976.

As the juniormost clerk, I had no real work for the eight months that I worked there. However, I did get to see a world very different from my own. I was attached to Mr Khuntia, an upper division clerk, as his understudy and assistant. He was a very conscientious person who wore a white dhoti, a spotless white long shirt and a pair of modest sandals. Like all other clerks, irrespective of age and seniority, I was also given the suffix 'babu'. Bagchi babu was now part of the system.

It was Khuntia babu who taught me one of the most important things for a clerk in any government office: how to open a file. When a letter arrives, it first has to be noted in a log maintained by the receipt and dispatch section. Then, based on the subject matter, it finds its way to a clerk and it is his task to give it life by opening a file in its honour. To file a letter, you first took a brown file cover called a file leaf. Then you put a coloured tag through a hole in the corner, gently punctured the letter and tagged it inside the file. Then you pierced the other end of the tag outside the file and attached a special paper inscribed with the words 'draft for approval'. This is the 'DFA sheet'—in government, acronyms convey a certain sense of officialese that the expanded form does not. On the DFA sheet, you wrote the draft of a reply as appropriate and sent it one step up the pyramid. As the file moves up, notations are made by the powers that be, either approving or disapproving the draft and sometimes conveying a decision that is called passing an order.

Like every soul on this earth has a body, every letter in the government must have a file. And every file has a number. Khuntia babu tended to his files like his own children, whom he saw only during the holidays because they lived in the village. Khuntia babu reported to Panda babu, the *bada babu* or sectional head clerk, a jovial man who clearly liked his job and his position. He had a dozen other clerks like Khuntia babu reporting to him.

In the industries department, there were three such teams of babus, each with a head clerk and a dedicated peon. Our group, chartered with looking after small-scale industries, had a tall peon whose family name was also Panda. He had the most monotonous job, which he did without complaint, or interest. He walked around barefoot, with a glazed look in his eyes. The department had a group of middle-aged clerks who actively discussed politics, sports and anything else, making the place both interesting and sometimes unproductive. That group laid claim on me as soon as I arrived and would occasionally call me in to be moderator or judge when rivals got into a deadlock over warring points of view. Conciliation often involved a trip to the staff canteen where tea, a small snack and a peace pipe signalled truce. All this meant I hung out with men twice my age, and they bought me tea or a snack and a cigarette or a paan. One day, while returning from the staff canteen after one such exercise, I was claimed by yet another group.

Panda, our peon, caught hold of my hand and in a hushed voice asked me to follow him. The secretariat building had four high-ceilinged floors and finally a massive roof. No one I knew ever went there. From the canteen, Panda took me to the topmost floor, opened a door and there, in a circle, sat a group of other peons. One look at them and you knew it was an exclusive club to which entry was strictly by invitation. The group looked up, took no great notice of me and Panda—no questions were asked, no introductions made; they merely shifted to make room for the two of us. It was the brotherhood of hash smokers. Every man took a long, appreciative drag from a *chillum* filled with grass that was passed around from one to another in a circular, silent ritual. Though I was not in the habit of smoking hash, I felt I could not let Panda down. So, when the stuff reached me, I took a symbolic drag, thereby acknowledging my acceptance of their affection for me. Though I never returned to the club, later in life I was to understand the power of communities in large places of work and how little management knows of their presence and their role. We only think of workers as work units, seldom realizing that people are like bees. Bees do not just go to their hives to work; they live there.

¤

The system knew that I was a transient. It never loaded me with any significant work. On top of that, I was attending law classes in the evening and through that connection continued to often represent the university in interstate debates. If a government employee participates in any national-level competition, be it academic or sports related, one can get almost unlimited time off. As a result, I was given weeks of special leave of absence. The days that I did come to work, Khuntia babu did not ask me to do much.

It was perhaps all because of a small task that was given to me soon after I joined. The secretary in the industries department, one of the dozen or so senior IAS officers who ran the state, had received an invitation to some inconsequential event which he wanted to decline. The instruction to decline the invitation flowed from him to the deputy secretary, to the under secretary, to the head clerk, to the dealing assistant Khuntia babu, who, in turn, finally asked me to put up a draft for approval that would go back the same way it had come and with or without changes, return the same way down again, to finally go to a typist who would then prepare the final letter for the secretary's signature.

I dutifully submitted my draft to Khuntia babu who forwarded it to Panda babu. After a while, I saw the two men hunched over my draft, with a rather foreboding expression on their faces. I knew I had blown it. After a while, the two men called me and with a mixture of apprehension and awkwardness, asked me the meaning of the opening sentence, 'Due to pressing preoccupations,

I will not be able to join you on this very happy occasion.'

The two men did not understand the term 'pressing preoccupations' and after getting me to explain it to them, they decided to drop it. A more suitable substitute was incorporated. In the process, I think, it was also settled between them that it would be better to keep me harmlessly engaged than load me with any real work that could end up creating more work for them. So I came and went as I pleased, attended to the occasional low-voltage errand, mediated the clerical wars on world affairs, attended staff picnics, went to many a fellow clerk's home for dinner. Towards the end, I even went along as a polling officer for the historic 1976 national elections even though I was not of voting age myself. Amidst all this, I filled my days and months with the hope that I would soon be some place else. What that place was, I did not know.

¤

In the large hall across the small industries section was the establishment section. There was no wall between the two sections; this led to borderless camaraderie between the clerks. Each section, like ours, had an intercom on the bada babu's table. But, there was only one telephone with a direct, external line to the world and it sat on the desk of the head clerk of the establishment section. He was a very committed and busy man called Ramakanta Pattanaik. I used to go to his desk because Susmita would call me on rare instances. As was the protocol, after the phone call visit to Pattanaik babu's desk, one had to stop to make small talk with some co-workers there before coming back to my section.

One of the senior clerks in the establishment section was the most efficient, hard-working, happy and punctual man in the entire department. His cheerfulness was contagious. Everyone liked him for his demeanour, his high energy and ever-smiling face. One day I saw him looking rather solemn and walked up to ask him if everything was all right. He looked very embarrassed that I had even noticed that there was something unusual about his demeanour. Quickly, trying to recover, he sought to dismiss my query. When I persisted, he told me that it had indeed been a rough week for him. His wife was admitted in a hospital in Cuttack for cancer treatment. He had to take care of the children at home, cook, come to work and then go to Cuttack at the end of the day to look after her.

'But that by itself is not a big deal for me, Bagchi babu. Though, of course, right now I also have to supervise the children's studies because they are having their examinations. I can still manage that. It's just that my old mother, who lives in the village, has chosen to visit us at this very time. Unfortunately, she is mentally ill.'

I stood looking at him in dead silence. I did not know what to say, or what to do. He looked visibly relieved that he had taken the opportunity to get it all off his chest, despite the awkwardness of having discussed it with someone who would not be able to make any difference to his life. He shifted his attention back to the work on hand and I slowly returned to my table, next to Khuntia babu, and slumped into my chair.

Someone once said, most men take more out of life than they give to it. A few give more to life than they take out of it. The world runs because of such men.

¤

By spring of the next year, time had begun to drag its feet. All my friends were pursuing the more proven path while I had jumped off from the train at an unknown junction, not knowing where I was going or when the next train would arrive. It created a sense of loneliness. I couldn't shake the feeling I was on the cusp of change. Studying law was just marking time. In Bhubaneswar, anyone could enroll for a law degree irrespective of educational competence. Working in the secretariat for two long years before I could sit for the civil services examination seemed like an endless tunnel. I needed a proper job. I needed a career, which was not the civil services because that meant waiting, being a burden on someone. And in any case, the civil services did not mean much to me. I kept applying for any job for which I could remotely justify my eligibility. So, when I saw an advertisement from the DCM group for management trainees, half unsure that they would even consider me with a political science degree, I applied. A few days later, I received a call. After a round of aptitude tests, group discussions and interviews at the regional level, I made it to the finals. I think what paved the path for me was the fact that the head of DCM's management training programme, Colonel Kucchal, probably liked the 'best NCC cadet' bit in my resumé. Maybe it was something else. After the final round of interviews at the regional level, I was told I needed to go to Delhi for the national-level selection.

My friend Anup Mohapatra lent me his jacket and a good shirt and a tie. DCM paid first-class train fare from Bhubaneswar to Delhi for me to attend the interview. I boarded the Utkal Express to Delhi with great expectations. It took two long days. From my first-class berth, I watched the world go past me as the train wound its way through the lush green forests of Madhya Pradesh and the ravines of the Chambal valley, past the vast fertile fields of Uttar Pradesh, past the historic city of Agra, to finally pull into Hazrat Nizamuddin Railway Station in posh south Delhi. Throughout the journey, I couldn't escape the feeling that I was being taken to where I would finally belong.

The final interview was conducted in an imposing boardroom at DCM's corporate office by the entire top management. Eighteen men, including Dr Bharat Ram and Dr Charat Ram, the two managing directors and heirs of the founder Lala Shriram, peered down at the candidates. The panel included Dr Bansi Dhar, deputy managing director, and the legendary Mr Dharma Vira, who as the erstwhile governor of West Bengal had sacked a chief minister named Ajoy

Mukherjee. My interview began with a conversation on the power of conflict. Soon it moved to a discussion on the theory of karma in the Bhagavad Gita and then to Hegelian dialectics. I felt it was my day; I was cruising.

I returned to Bhubaneswar; the offer to join the DCM group as a management trainee arrived in the post. Being selected was seen as a great achievement. The DCM group ran one of the most coveted management trainee schemes in the country and paid rather well. The starting salary was more than three times what I was earning as a lower division clerk. Armed with the trunk my father had given me when I was a schoolboy, a few hundred rupees arranged by Amitav, a basic set of clothes and old bedding, I took a train to New Delhi to report for work. I had been assigned to Delhi Cloth Mills—the oldest textile mill in the group. Located in the shabby area of Bara Hindu Rao, it sat between what is New Delhi and Old Delhi. The road in front of the mill started from Bara Hindu Rao on one end and went towards Kishen Gunj, where many of the millhands lived in dilapidated, low-cost housing. People on the road jostled with horse-drawn carriages, pushcarts, makeshift tea stalls and squatters. During the change of shift, thousands of workers would pour in and out, many dressed in no more than striped long underwear and a *fatua*, a compromise between an undershirt and a shirt with a pocket in the front to keep the attendance card, small change and some chewing tobacco. The air was thick with vehicle exhaust, the smell of horse and cow dung, beedi smoke and communism. One look at the place was enough to make a true-blue, pedigreed MBA run away. But I wasn't true blue and pedigreed and the secretariat in Bhubaneswar had prepared me well to feel quite at home in a non-glamorous setting. Delhi Cloth Mills, my workplace for the next five years, was a far cry from the opulent boardroom where I had been interviewed but relevant to the discussion on Hegelian dialectics in a somewhat convoluted manner.

I started my training in the time office. At the gate of the mill, at the blast of the siren, thousands of workmen, some barefoot, some semi-clad, would march in with their attendance cards in hand. They had the smell of beedi and sweat from the previous day's work and their struggle for food and sleep in the ghetto-like worker's colony. They handed over the attendance cards to clerks with thick glasses sliding down their noses. The clerks sat under whirring fans black with accumulated soot. They marked the workers' struggle for yet another day, payable as wages, in a large register.

After learning how the time office worked, I shifted to the pay office where the wages were calculated, then I went to train on the shop floor where the bales of cotton became spun yarn, learnt how they were woven into warps and wefts before being dyed and printed and then cut into metres of cloth that would be packed in bales to be transported to hundreds of destinations, before finding their place in retail showrooms that flaunted neon DCM signs, to eventually drape a nation. For an entire year, I worked in various departments of the factory. I also learnt the demand side from a more sophisticated marketing department that generated the indents, housed outside the factory in air-conditioned offices. I went to see how actual trade took place in the bylanes or sarais of Chandni Chowk in Delhi where wholesalers and retailers haggled, cheated each other, worked and laughed together. In between, they ate hot samosas and *matthi*, and drank *banta*, a soda drink in a bottle with a marble ball in its neck that made a mini explosion when opened.

After just a few months on the job, management trainee salaries were further revised. I was now earning one thousand eight hundred rupees a month—six times what I had made in the government. My friends were still in college and here I was remitting money home dutifully every month. I used to address the money-order form to my mother and each time the receipt came back signed by her, I marvelled at the steady signature that masked the fact that she was actually a woman whose eyesight had been permanently robbed by destiny.

¤

What similarities exist between the days that I spent at the secretariat and those that I live at MindTree today? How does the work there resemble my work here? Or for that matter, does the world in which I live and work at this stage of my career even remotely resemble the sights, sounds and smells of Kishen Gunj, off Bara Hindu Rao, Delhi, 1977?

Our lives are like rivers—the source seldom reveals the confluence. Does a river fret over the long journey and about its end just as it is about to spurt? It simply does not do that, caring instead to flow, to begin its journey, and on its way builds a beneficial relationship with anyone who comes in contact with her.

CHAPTER 7

Killer, Get Killed

After a year of on-the-job training, a management trainee was designated as an officer on special duty. This involved becoming an understudy to a senior manager and some real work. I was asked to report to Mahesh Chand Bahree who was the works secretary of the Delhi Cloth Mills.

On my arrival in his office, I was greeted with a mixture of warmth and apprehension.

'Sonny boy,' said Mahesh Chand Bahree, adjusting his trademark dark glasses and thrusting his big chest forward, 'my principle in life is: Killer, get killed.'

Bahree was a powerful man who had come up in life the hard way. Starting life as a textile engineer, he had lost one eye when a spindle had gone right through it on the shop floor. After that accident, he was given administrative work and he now looked after a wide range of commercial functions. The man was extremely knowledgeable and competent. But at some level, he was also insecure. Someone had told him that I had been made his understudy to eventually replace him. The principle about elimination of a potential adversary which he greeted me with was in that context.

But I liked the man. He had a certain aura, an earthy charm and undeniable competence. Above all, he treated 'small people'—drivers, peons, loaders—with respect and camaraderie. He spoke to illiterate workmen in their language, cracked jokes with them, but pulled them up when required. He knew each and every worker's family background. His knowledge of government regulations made even government officials treat him with respect. He did not have children and I missed my father. So, when he used to call me 'sonny boy', I loved it. After a few weeks of working with each other, he became comfortable enough to lower his guard and I ignored the veiled threat he had held out on the first day. We became a great team.

Every morning, even before the siren would signal the start of the general shift at 9 a.m., I would pull into the parking lot on my brand new Yezdi motorcycle, pretending it was a Mig-21 fighter aircraft, to see Mahesh Bahree already waiting there. He always arrived before me. A big man, he dressed carefully to appear casual and irreverent. Towards that end, he wore a bush shirt and never tucked it in. His overall demeanour would have qualified him to be a general in any army.

Mahesh Bahree was never alone. Even at that early hour, there would be a couple of people around him. It could be a worker who was on his way to the spinning department, an excise inspector, a colleague from marketing or a security guard. What fascinated me was how they were all attracted to his presence, and as they stood casually chatting with him for two, five or ten minutes, he was actually debriefing them. Mahesh Bahree knew everything that was going on in the mill, all the time.

After I had safely manoeuvred the make-believe Mig-21 into a parking position and taken my flight helmet off, the big man and the boy-man would make a round of the factory. He had two alternative starting points for the walking tour. Either we would begin at the cotton godown or at the coal yard—they were at two ends of the vast smoke-stack factory, separated by a few kilometres. Between the two points was the unending shop floor that converted cotton into yarn, yarn into woven cloth, dyed the woven cloth in different colours, printed it, sized and packed the bales before stacking them in the warehouse. This warehouse was Mahesh Bahree's territory. So was the coal yard. The factory could not depend on the irregular supply of electricity from the Delhi Electric Supply Undertaking, a government undertaking. Coal was required to generate power and steam that the plant needed for certain operations. The supply of coal had three government agencies involved— Coal India that mined the coal, the Railway Board that cated the wagons for transporting the coal and the zonal railway departments that brought the coal from the mines to the plant. It was a difficult combination to manage and the plant always remained hand to mouth in the supply of coal. If the coal did not arrive on time, the cotton was useless. It was Mahesh Bahree's job to ensure that the coal yard was always full. The godown where the cotton was stored did not come directly under his purview, but its load level told him how much coal was required. At any point of time, he knew what the marketing forecast was and what the cotton stock actually looked like, and then he did the math in his head on how much coal his men needed to arrange for. He could have read the MIS report on his table; his job did not require him to walk to the coal yard and cotton godown every day. But he preferred getting his information hands-on.

During the one hour walking tour every morning, Mahesh Bahree would acknowledge a steady stream of greetings. With some he would exchange a few words, with others he would share a joke, and some he would acknowledge with merely a grunt. If any of the recipients was a character of significance, he would tell me all about the person and what to expect of him. He was like a big burly bear teaching his younger one the ways of the jungle.

¤

Like many great men, Mahesh Bahree too had an Achilles' heel. He had a soft corner for one of his section heads who took undue advantage of his proximity to the boss.

The man had a group of assistants under him, who were themselves very indisciplined and unionized. Bahree, inexplicably, tolerated them right under his nose. Instead of working, Bahree's favourite section head used to loiter, run errands for Bahree and sometimes just sit in front of him doing nothing. As fate would have it, the group was asked to report to me. The section head was used to working directly under Bahree and thought I was a notional boss who would simply humour him. He had no idea that I disliked my subordinate hanging out with my boss as his primary activity, day in and day out. I did not play ball and tension began to brew. Things came to a head one day when he made disparaging remarks about the company's management in front of a visitor in my presence. He was the boss's man and much older to me, but I was not going to take this lying down. I demanded that he be transferred from the department to the shop floor for his inappropriate remarks unless he apologized to me. Mahesh Bahree was in an awkward situation. He referred the matter to his boss. Having taken a stand, I had to see things through to their logical end. I informed my bosses that they had twenty-four hours within which to transfer the man out or else I would be putting in my papers. When the deadline expired, I submitted my resignation.

The prospect of unemployment loomed large. I spoke to Amitav and told him what had happened. Still struggling to get his own professional toehold and barely able to make both ends meet, he simply said, 'Come singing back.'

Life sometimes deals you a blank cheque. However, it pays to defer its encashment. Rather than return to Bhubaneswar, I decided to wait for the system to respond. Next morning, the phone on my desk rang. I was being called to the new executive director's room.

CHAPTER 8

In the Path of Jupiter

The DCM group had diversified into chemicals, rayon, foundry, computers, automotive and many other businesses. In addition, there were a whole bunch of businesses like electrical equipment and refrigeration under the Shriram name. The DCM group had originated with the pioneering efforts of an industrialist, Lala Shriram, who was no more. His two sons, Dr Bharat Ram and Dr Charat Ram, owned the various businesses with clear demarcation between them. Both were very different people, with vastly different leadership styles. Dr Bharat Ram's businesses included textiles and within that, among several mills, was Delhi Cloth Mills. It was the mother unit set up by Lala Shriram. However, it was also in a state of decay that no one seemed to be able to stem. When I joined in 1977, there was a young and dynamic general manager named H.N. Chaturvedi. Despite all his efforts, things only got worse. Into my second year, the owners decided to bring in Brihaspati Dev Pathak to replace Chaturvedi. Pathak, who was in charge of the rayon business, had been with the company since the days of Lala Shriram, had shown great calibre and was trusted by all the family members. He had the reputation of having successfully run Delhi Cloth Mills at one time and it was felt that he could turn things around.

Brihaspati Dev Pathak had arrived amidst much hope and fear—hope for a turnaround, fear for what may happen if it didn't. As a sign of respect, he was addressed as 'Pathakji' by everyone. Cynics, however, called him 'paon choo Pathak', alluding to his love for people to bow down and touch his feet as a mark of sycophancy when he moved around the factory. He was also known to listen to a group of cronies, had a flaming temper, a pronounced hatred for smoking and alcohol and, some said, Punjabi managers. Mahesh Chand Bahree was a smoker, enjoyed his drinks in the privacy of his own home, made no bones about it and was a Punjabi.

Pathak was a freckled, small, old man, but had the energy of a bull. Once, on a trip with him to see the rayon plant at Kota, Rajasthan, he invited me to stay in his house. He ran his business like a spiritual dictator. While driving to Kota, his driver suddenly braked because a cat crossed the car's path. That is considered a bad omen in any part of India. If a cat crosses the road, most drivers stop, back up a few yards and then start again to neutralize any evil. When his driver did this, Pathak admonished the driver, dramatically adding, 'Don't stop the car. Let the cat wonder whose path she was trying to cross today.'

Having made up my mind to leave DCM rather than cower in front of my boss's sidekick, I was now sitting across Brihaspati Dev Pathak, a man more than three times my age and in the ultimate position of power. After listening to my explanation, all he asked was, 'Have you ever seen a seed sprouting from under a big boulder?'

'Yes, sir.'

'When the seed is under the huge rock, who has the upper hand, the greater power?'

'The rock, sir.'

'Precisely. The relative balance of power is in favour of the rock. The rock can crush the sapling. The sapling, however, does not assert itself, does not fight the rock; it gently circumvents the rock and keeps growing along its side. And one day, that same sapling has become a huge tree. At that time, where do you think the rock sits?'

I kept quiet.

'It remains at the feet of the tree forever.'

The message was clear. As a sapling, I was choosing to fight the rock. Pathak wanted me to circumvent it. I took back my resignation, walked to the errant man's desk and gave him a hug.

¤

Pathak's taking over the plant resulted in no magical turnaround. Workers, staff and managers became more political; gossip and backbiting multiplied like lice. Then the textile unions in Delhi gave a call for a strike, demanding a total relook at the prevailing wages. The management of the already bleeding Delhi Cloth Mills decided to take the issue head-on and all negotiations failed. Six thousand factory workers went on strike. It was an unusual experience for me to see a lockout declared in a factory. With spying and counter-spying, there was a deadlock between management and workers. The workers took turns to sit in front of the main gate as a sign of protest. Days turned into weeks and soon it was clear that the strike may even last six months. The company was running out of cash, there were prior sales obligations and unmet export commitments while thousands of bales of cloth lay inside the mill. A court order allowed the company to move out all the finished goods but the question was how to take them out while the unions blocked the main gate?

Mahesh Bahree suggested moving trucks to the coal yard behind the plant and moving the bales of cloth out through a back gate at night. No union worker would bother to go there. I was assigned to supervise the movement of goods under cover of darkness. It would have been quite possible but for the long distance between the finished goods warehouse and the coal yard and the only way of moving the cloth bales was to use manual labour. The effort was so huge that after one night we were able to move out only a couple of small truckloads.

We gave up the idea. More than twenty truckloads of finished goods were waiting inside to be evacuated.

The only option that now remained was to storm the front gate, take the picketing workers by total surprise and clear the goods from the warehouse before the workers realized what was going on. The workers' colony was some distance from the mill. The predicted response when the picketing workers discovered what was happening would be to run to the colony to bring other workmen, their spouses and children and create a human blockade that would not allow the trucks to leave. That could lead to violence. The police were willing to cooperate with us on one condition. They would give us protection, for just one hour, but if anything went wrong, they would not use force against the striking workers.

Mahesh Bahree was willing to take the gamble but it required a reconnaissance trip inside the plant to plan the minute-by-minute manoeuvre. It had to be foolproof. We only had this one chance for success. Bahree could not be seen anywhere near the factory as every picketing worker would recognize him. I volunteered to go in there dressed as a security officer. The law guaranteed full protection to the plant's security personnel. It was at once a daring and a juvenile plan. If the trick failed, I could get lynched. Anything could happen thereafter. Mahesh Bahree thought for a while and gave me the go-ahead.

The very next day an official-looking car pulled up in front of the main gate with me dressed in khaki uniform, sunglasses and a peaked cap pulled over my face. The strikers gave contemptuous looks and went about their game of cards. I was inside.

On the designated day, twenty trucks escorted by the Delhi Police moved in. There was one hitch though. The police had guaranteed us protection for one hour only inside the premises. Once the loaded convoy was out of the gate, they could not give protection; it was a risk the management would have to bear. The story went that in another mill striking workers had run after the last vehicle of a convoy and set it on fire. That was a real possibility, of people jumping on to the last truck and resorting to arson. It was too late to worry about that risk now, but I sensed that it created fear in the minds of the truckers. Who would be willing to be the tail of the convoy? I looked them in the eye and said I would be on the last truck—not with the driver in his cabin. I would ride in the back. A cheer went up, the truckers jostled to be the last so they could have Bagchi saab as their *khalasi*, the driver's sidekick who sometimes rides the load.

The operation was completed, not giving enough time for the strikers to react in numbers. The convoy rolled out. It was the first and last time I had the privilege of sitting on the back of a loaded truck riding the roads of Delhi.

Mahesh Bahree's greatness was in trusting a twenty-two-year-old management trainee with an operation whose success was less than certain. He taught me to take risks, to allow people the freedom to try things out without the fear of consequences.

¤

After what looked like eternity, the strike was finally called off. However, when the factory opened, we had an unusual set of problems on our hands. On the one hand, there were no fresh stocks; on the other, huge loads of unsold cloth were lying in far-flung places which had not been lifted by the dealers who had taken advantage of the strike to go back on some of their obligations. When the factory opened, it was now necessary to bring these goods back and liquidate the inventory to raise working capital. Some of it was needed on an emergency basis. Bahree was asked to move truckloads of cloth bales lying in Calcutta. Unfortunately, there was a shortage of trucks. The private operator who ran the Calcutta route demanded his pound of flesh and though we had an ongoing contract, citing that it covered shipment and not return, demanded a different tariff. Bahree went to the negotiation table and agreed to a tariff hike. The goods were brought back but word went around that the transport company had actually brought the bales back in railway wagons instead of using their trucks even though they had negotiated a higher transport charge for returning the goods by road. Whether the rumour was true or not, this was Pathak's moment to put Bahree in the dock. I was Bahree's assistant and Pathak needed me to testify that Bahree had compromised his official position and, in fact, was hand in glove with the transport agency. As I stood before Brihaspati Dev Pathak, he read out the charge he wanted to level against Bahree and asked me, in effect, to be the approver. If I corroborated even mildly, I could aspire to get my boss's job.

I looked the man in the eye and told him that at best there might have been an executive error in judgement during the negotiations but there could never be the slightest doubt about Mahesh Bahree's integrity—his character was unimpeachable. Pathak's eyes conveyed only one thing: that I was a traitor; I had crossed over to the side of the already condemned.

Bahree was sacked and I was transferred to the marketing department where I sat in a room with no windows and three clerks outside to look after some very inconsequential commercial tasks. No one visited; the phone on my desk never rang. During lunch, I would read the *Economic Times* cover to cover. This was also the year I had married Susmita, and she was still at the university completing her master's. We ran our little world on a shoestring budget. As if things were not bad enough at work, I was hospitalized twice in quick succession for typhoid and to top it all the doctors discovered that I had irisitis in my left eye. It was a rare condition that had reduced the vision to 6/60 and I was being injected with steroids in my eye. Due to the prolonged hospitalization, I had run out of all my accumulated leave. The only man who could grant me special leave so that I did not have to suffer loss of pay was Pathak. I went to meet him with my eye in bandage. The man who had hosted me at his house in Kota and had counselled me to withdraw my resignation looked at me as if I was a worm and dismissed me saying it wasn't the responsibility of the company to take care of my vision. I would not be paid my salary for that month.

In addition to the fall from grace, I was now in the unenviable position of being completely isolated. I knew that everyone was watching with the knowledge that my time was over. With Mahesh Bahree gone, I was directly in the path of Jupiter's storm. People who once admired me were now looking at me with sympathy.

¤

A man named Arie de Geus who started his working life with Royal Dutch Shell is an important management thinker of our times. He and his colleagues at Royal Dutch Shell worked for many years on the now famous concept of Scenario Planning—a tool embraced by large corporations, military and development strategists alike. Peter Senge, author of *The Fifth Discipline* and later, *Presence*, credits him with the concept of the learning organization. Arie de Geus, in his book *The Living Company*, alludes to organizations as living things. Living things are characterized by their capacity to remember. With this, we build memories. But few understand that we are not only capable of creating memories of our past, we can actually create memories of the future. The human mind, confronted with decisions, is trained to stay with the familiar. Thus even when we are faced with seemingly unfamiliar situations in life and make choices that seem to come from nowhere, in reality, they stem from memories of the future. In some ways, I was to leave DCM behind and in many ways I would carry it forward. Meanwhile the tipping point of my life awaited me, just round the bend.

PART II

CHAPTER 9

Learning to Fly

By the spring of 1981 it had become quite clear to me that I had to move out of DCM. Unfortunately, a five-year stint in plant administration was not exactly the most marketable work experience. When I scoured the newspapers, most job opportunities seemed to be in the areas of finance or marketing. My experience was irrelevant to both. The occasional administration manager's job required a forty-year-old and I was not even twenty-four!

A mentor within the system suggested that I move to the computer division of the DCM group that manufactured microprocessor-based systems. It was easier said than done. There were solid walls between DCM's different divisions and you needed a godfather to scale them. Around the same time, someone suggested that I meet Anil Dang, an export manager, who, as his reporting line was different, was outside Jupiter's path. Maybe he could help. Being an ex-management trainee himself, he was sympathetic when I met him. He thought the idea of seeking an internal transfer from one DCM unit to another was futile. He suggested that I explore employment possibilities with a start-up named HCL. He knew the founders there. Specifically, he was willing to give me an introduction to the head of human resources, a man named George Koreth.

When I met Koreth, he gave me two pieces of information: the only position HCL was hiring for was entry-level salespeople and that the guaranteed monthly salary would be 40 per cent lower than what DCM was paying me at the time. There was the possibility of earning commission on sales, but that income would be variable and, in fact, it would take a year to determine how much commission I had earned. This meant that for at least a year Susmita and I would have serious cash flow problems. She was still at college and, occasionally, we also needed to send some money home.

There was a third angle to the whole dilemma: the distance I would have to commute every day would be four times what I was used to and that meant increased fuel costs.

But there were silver linings to the cloud. Switching over to sales would allow me to learn new job skills, and give me a new life away from the politics of a decadent, smoke-stack system that had already condemned me to the electric chair. If I made enough sales calls using my own motorbike every day, the mileage reimbursements for that could cover the cost of the extra commute as well.

The key question in all this then really was—was I ready to take a 40 per cent cut in salary?

Sometimes, in our moments of conflict, we come across a sign that, in a flash, helps us reach a decision which hours of frustrating reasoning cannot achieve. Almost magically options become clear. One evening, while walking in Connaught Circus, I saw a book with a rather unusual cover. It showed a bird in flight, wings outstretched. The book was *Jonathan Livingston Seagull* by Richard Bach. Impulsively, I bought the book and began reading it as soon as I reached home. I couldn't put it down once I started reading. The protagonist of the book, Jonathan Livingston Seagull, taught me that life's true purpose is not to live to earn; it's about having the courage to take flight. Susmita also read the book and, suddenly, the decision we had to take was clear— we would take the risk, a leap into the future. Cash flow became unimportant. If I did well, we would be able to make up the loss in income through sales commissions. If I did not, it didn't matter. We would figure things out. After all, in another year, she would have completed her studies and could get a job.

I resigned from DCM; the system quietly accepted it. My staff gave me a loving, private farewell and I crossed over from a company that had started in the nineteenth century to one that had a toehold in the twenty-first. On

1 July 1981 I reported for work at HCL's spartan office in Nehru Place, New Delhi and the first thing I realized was that I knew nothing about computers or about selling.

¤

Like Jonathan Livingston Seagull's initial flights which were very rough, my early days at HCL were uncomfortable too. Jonathan learnt to soar and glide and dive and catch a thermal only after some time; it took me a while to adjust to life as a door-to-door salesman. But soon, there was no looking back. For the next three decades, the ever-changing world of computers and computer technology beckoned and fascinated me. And for all this, I have only one man to thank— Brihaspati Dev Pathak.

I learnt the basics of selling at HCL from my boss R.K. Gupta. Every morning he would give me a prospect list, and I spent the whole day going from one office to another, trying to convince people to buy a two-floppy-drive computer with 64KB memory, a display unit and a dot-matrix printer for nearly four lakhs! Sometimes, I made complete cold calls on potential first-time users, small businessmen who ran a factory or a wholesale trading business. Occasionally, my calls were to medium-sized enterprises and, quite often, to government departments.

I worked for HCL very briefly. Though I liked the informality of the place, the company did not have the level of customer focus that I felt was required. We were focussing on the first-time user segment of the market, and that required a tremendous amount of hand-holding. Frustrated with the company's aggressive selling style and low customer focus, a dozen or so of us moved away to join PSI Data Systems headquartered in Bangalore. It was a start-up that had remained low-key for years but was now revamping its operations with fresh capital infusion and was keen to hire new talent.

During my years at PSI, I sold computers in Delhi and places like Jaipur, Udaipur, Lucknow, Rae Bareilly. I visited many dusty little towns, travelling there on my bike, by train, by auto-rickshaws hired for the day and by bus. It was great training for me because in a management career a sales job is a great way to reach the top. PSI turned out to be a wonderful place to learn because of its R&D capability. The company had been co-founded by two Stanford graduates, Dr V.K. Ravindran and Vinay Deshpande, who believed there was scope for and need to create private sector R&D in India. At that time, the Indian navy had several third-generation missile control systems on board its ships based on Digital's PDP/11 technology. The US government was controlling the export of such technology because of the cold war and India's political proximity to the USSR. A few scientists in the Department of Electronics were aware of PSI's R&D capabilities and entrusted it with developing indigenous PDP/11 technology so that India did not have to be at the mercy of the United States. This led to the creation of a new line of computers at PSI. But despite PSI's great R&D, the company was not commercially successful with its line of products. A time came when the company went into default in paying salaries to its employees. Satrajit Majumdar, head of sales and marketing at PSI, was hired by MMC Digital Systems, a computer company started by the Mahindras. He asked me to come along to work with him as a product manager—this meant a departure from pure sales into marketing for me. Despite my reasonably successful migration into sales, I felt I was cerebrally more tuned to product management and also wanted the experience of a staff assignment—working for a senior executive in a corporate role as against a frontline job like selling. However, my stint at MMC ended barely a year after I joined because the company was wound up. The management had underestimated the amount of investment required and lacked staying power. Further, the senior management of the company was drawn from the textile machinery manufacturing businesses of the group; they were unable to understand the chaotic rhythm of the IT business.

¤

My early years at HCL, PSI and MMC taught me sales and marketing; these years became a solid foundation for my stints in international business much later. No other profession teaches you the true worth of your own abilities than a sales job. The reason is simple: the outcome is completely binary. Either you have made a sale or you have not.

In no other profession are you required to listen as much. A salesperson must not only listen with his mind, he has to sometimes listen with his soul. You learn to read body language and emotions. You learn to isolate the stated needs from the unstated concerns of a customer. Only when you listen well, are you able to see what lies beneath the surface. Like an iceberg, nine-tenths of a customer's needs and requirements are hidden below the surface of what he is telling you as you are pitching your product. A good salesperson learns to understand and address these.

In sales, one learns to deal with a variety of people. No two customers or methods of selling are the same. One day I could be selling to an extremely well-informed research director at the Railway Design & Standards Organization at Lucknow. The next day, I could be selling to a barely literate, small factory owner in west Delhi or a chartered accountant in Udaipur. Each customer is strikingly different from the other.

Even as you meet the same customers many times over a sales cycle, you see them in different moods and moments. They can be very different people, depending on whether it is the first call, the final negotiation or in the meeting just after the trial balloon has collapsed during the pilot phase of a large, multi-year contract.

Selling and negotiation skills are intertwined. A sale without a negotiation is like courtship without romance. The negotiation skills we learn in selling become essential as one grows in any profession. You negotiate with your boss, your peers, your children and sometimes with complete strangers. While life is about constant negotiation, only selling teaches you the nuances of negotiating.

A salesperson learns to take rejection as a way of life. Sometimes, a customer can be downright abusive. Yet, good salespeople learn that the real meaning of a 'No' is 'Not now'.

A salesperson gets to know the real face of his organization and its capabilities, to taste, first-hand, the truth about the company's products and services. He knows how good his customer service teammates are and what is the true capability of the support functions. A proud salesperson is always the product of a great company. If you can get under the hood and determine whether a salesperson has genuine respect for his company, be assured that the organization is good and worth doing business with.

In selling, you get to truly appreciate the value of building a network, of cultivating friendships with people even when you do not have an immediate need for them. Any good salesperson will tell you how much he values his rolodex and what he does to keep in touch with the people he knows.

When selling, you learn that every buyer need not be a favour-seeking, corrupt person. How often do you find that it is the salesperson that first uses unfair means to get ahead; a corruptible buyer looks for signals of connivance. Yet, when you do not respond favourably, the other party may still be willing to do business with you, despite your unwillingness to grease palms.

The traditional responsibility of a CEO is managing resources like men, material, money and information. Additionally, today's CEO must learn how to manage complexity and be a first-rate rainmaker. If the CEO can sell well, the entire organization follows suit. For this, nothing trains you better than life in the trenches: good, solid, hard work in the early part of your career.

¤

Selling wasn't the only thing I learnt during my early years in the computer industry. I was also privileged to meet a set of brilliant people who were quietly laying the foundations of the industry in their own different ways. One such individual was Pradeep Gupta who had started *Dataquest*, India's longest-running computer magazine. From time to time, he asked me to contribute articles. Later, it was *Dataquest* that offered me my first column called 'A Little Beyond'; this brought me instant recognition in the industry. From writing one column, over the years, I wrote two more for *Dataquest*. This led to writing in other newspapers and periodicals.

I began to realize the importance of writing in my regular work as well. Communication is a key requirement to be an effective leader in a large organization. Those who write well, learn to synthesize their ideas better; it makes them better thinkers. Leaders who generate content even as they perform their work, help their organizations learn. They are able to create alignment with larger groups of people within and inclusion with the world outside. Affection for content helps to build and disseminate points of view effectively. Like a sport, writing requires cultivation over a long period of time and can become a fulfilling occupation. Even today, writing remains my most serious passion outside work.

We all have some talent in us—be it singing, writing, painting or sculpting. If we nuture and cherish it, it makes our life fuller. Yet so many of us choose the uni-dimensionality of a work life, always citing lack of time to pursue a hobby. If we make a small commitment towards keeping our talent alive, one day it becomes a beautiful gift, which nourishes us, makes our lives complete.

CHAPTER 10

Learning to Fail

The early days of the Indian computer industry were far from the hustle and bustle that we associate with it today. In the 1980s, the software industry was practically non-existent. We had a hard time explaining to people the meaning of software—the concept was too abstract. The only worthwhile player in the software services business was Tata Consultancy Services (TCS). Companies like Wipro and HCL, which have become synonymous with software today, provided software services simply to earn dollars through exports so that they could import chips and peripherals to assemble and sell hardware (computers) in India. Software in that sense wasn't their true calling.

By 1985, when MMC decided to pretty much close

down its computer business, once again my professional career was at a crossroads. The country's annual computer offtake could be counted in the hundreds. What MMC had not realized was that with Rajiv Gandhi becoming prime minister, the computer industry was destined to see explosive growth in just a couple of years. Sometimes success is just so close, it looks unreal.

It was around this time I got my first taste of entrepreneurship. Satrajit Majumdar, my boss at MMC, and his friend Sujit Bose, formerly of IBM, who was at the time working for a pharmaceutical company, invited me to join them as co-founder of a business they were soon going to start. They were very different people—Satrajit was a corporate maverick, Sujit Bose an intellectual—but they shared a common belief that the time had come for an IT-related training organization for the corporate sector. There was a huge need for such an organization and there were hardly any competitors because NIIT, the largest in the training space, primarily focussed on training individuals and not companies. I seemed to have a natural flair for teaching, reading and writing and the invitation from two much older and experienced professionals was flattering. The idea of becoming my own master at the age of twenty-eight was too great an allure to miss.

I do not know how Susmita supported this idea. We had no savings, lived in a rented house, our older daughter Neha was three years old and our younger daughter Niti was born just a few days after our company, Project.21, got off the ground. Satrajit Majumdar and

Sujit Bose pooled about twenty thousand rupees between the two of them and agreed that I could pay for my part of the equity from the monthly salary I would earn. Satrajit had an uncle, whom everyone called Mama. Mama ran a small cardboard-tube factory atop a dilapidated building on Lower Circular Road in Calcutta. The old man was more curious than confident about what his nephew was up to and agreed that if his nephew paid cash upfront, he would build a ten foot by ten foot extension to his two-room factory. He would also allow us to use his phone subject to prompt payment and we could ask the woman who served tea to his dozen workmen to give us some too, but our account with her would have to be maintained separately. This was a fabulous arrangement because we could not afford anything better. Most banks we had approached had not even agreed to open a current account so that we could run the business, forget about giving us a line of credit, as we had no collateral to offer.

Project.21 began business on 1 April 1985. After struggling for a few months, the first desktop computer arrived. It was my responsibility to create the course material and manage the business in eastern India along with Suren Rasaily, an IIM-A alumnus, Ajith Madhavan, a young commerce graduate from Kerala who was trying to propagate computer literacy in remote corners of Rajasthan and Naren Mukherjee who had worked with me in MMC. Satrajit Majumdar started operations in Delhi with Gautam Rajkhowa, an ex-MMC colleague. Rakesh Madan, an ex-PSI colleague, started the Bangalore office and Ravi Madhavan, an IIM alumnus, started the Bombay branch. In all, we were about two dozen people. There was an egalitarian distribution of work—everyone pitched in from getting new clients, collecting the money, running to the bank, bundling course material, and even carting computers from place to place. Project.21 got noticed for its good work and a lot of business poured in. We trained people working in the coalfields of Madhya Pradesh for Coal India, in the oilfields in Tripura for ONGC, steel industry consultants MECON, and executives at Tata Steel and Chloride India became our regular clients.

¤

As is the case with most start-ups in their early years, Project.21 either had no business or too much work to handle. Cash flow remained a perpetual problem—the key was to look for an opportunity which would ensure steady revenue so that the future could be planned. This opportunity for Project.21 came when we pitched to handle Wipro's training requirement for their soon-to-be-launched personal computer (PC) range called the Little Genius. Indian organizations were unfamiliar with distributed or desktop computing; PCs were too expensive and were not really 'personal'. Wipro was thus positioning the Little Genius as a departmental machine. As a result, end users in large corporations needed to be trained to use it. Wipro was looking to offer three days of training for two people for every PC sold and wanted to outsource this assignment on a nationwide basis to consultants who would impart the training.

Project.21 was shortlisted to make a final presentation and I went to Bangalore to make it. That was the first time I met Ashok Soota. Anal Jain, vice president at Wipro, once told me that after the presentation on that day Ashok had asked why Wipro could not recruit me. Little did he know then that our paths were destined to converge and how!

Project.21 won the assignment and rolled out a nationwide training programme for Wipro. It brought all of us some financial relief for a brief while at least. But after three years it was becoming clear to me that we lacked two critical things to consolidate the company—we were underfunded and, more severely, as co-founders we lacked a shared vision. Project.21 had no working capital arrangements. Growth-bound start-ups need capital to run operations; they cannot be held hostage to fluctuating operational cash flow. Satrajit, Sujit and I focussed on different things for the growth trajectory of the organization. Satrajit loved the idea of running a business but soon got disenchanted with the nature of the training business and wanted to get into trading hardware in Russia. He felt there was more money and chances of immediate financial success in it. For Sujit Bose, Project.21 was a hobby, though a serious one. But you just cannot treat a start-up as your hobby, however passionate you may be about it. Start-ups are like children; in their infancy they need undivided attention. Amidst all this, Sujit Bose had also started a software company in association with a publishing house and that became his primary focus. Unable to solve the working capital problem, he tied in an equity deal with a data processing company, and we had two directors from this company on our board. They had expectations that Project.21 would help open doors for their data processing business with our clients. As soon as they realized this was not going to happen, they became disenchanted as well. Soon disagreements surfaced, money ran dry and things became difficult for everyone. Being young and immature, I invariably found myself in the middle.

Instinctively, however, I knew this was no way to run a business and decided it was time to return to regular employment within the industry. But before moving on, I wanted to see that my team was not left in the lurch as a result of Project.21's uncertain future. I spoke with Amit Dutta Gupta, a long-time mentor. He knew Rajendra Pawar, the man behind NIIT. I approached Rajendra. For NIIT, it was a great opportunity to acquire a first-rate team. The entire Project.21 team in Calcutta found jobs with NIIT. Bidding goodbye to my team, I went in search of my own destiny.

Between the occasional failure to pay the rent and the exhilaration on the faces of our clients, I loved the three years I spent at Project.21. They gave me the heady intoxication of being on my own, despite the fact that the company did not ever become big. The experience grounded me as an entrepreneur, taught me the pitfalls of running a start-up, and helped me learn what it takes to be a successful entrepreneur. It also taught me how to sell consulting, which is an abstract concept. Not everyone can sell and execute a consulting project—it requires something more than just knowledge and skill. Project.21 was meant to be a seed in my mind that would germinate exactly a decade later when the reason and season would come together. Meanwhile, I had more to learn.

CHAPTER 11

Winning the Mind Game

Most start-up companies anywhere in the world fail within the first year of their operation. They seldom fail because of financial reasons. They fail because the founders part ways. From a customer acquisition point of view, Project.21 had run fairly successfully for three years and it was a pity that we could not make it work. Parting is always fraught with a certain amount of blame, loss of relationship and a feeling of sadness. Yet, it is important to recognize that it is not healthy to cling to a dysfunctional arrangement.

In 1988, with Project.21 behind me, I once again began searching for a job. It is a fact of professional life that as you gain in seniority it becomes more difficult to find a good fit between yourself, the organization of your choice and the available role in it. I realized this in the course of interviews with a couple of organizations. My job search brought me to Bangalore. Being there, I decided to pay a courtesy call on Anal Jain at Wipro. It was meant to be just that. But as soon as he realized that I was looking for a change, he suggested that I consider Wipro. One thing led to another and before I knew it he had set up meetings with Ashok Soota, president of Wipro Information Technology and Azim Premji, chairman of Wipro Corporation. Within the next twenty-four hours, I had a job offer in hand. The job on the face of it was not glamorous. In fact, one could call it mundane, after the heady exhilaration of being an entrepreneur.

Wipro was considered a well-run company, its key players were all in place and almost all its managers were home grown. Traditionally, the company had been a mini-computer manufacturer that built custom applications as well as computers for large corporations. When it entered the PC business, its sourcing department, the factory and the sales reps in the field were quite unfamiliar with the problem of scale. Mini-computers were high-margin products shipped in hundreds; PCs were low-margin products that had to be shipped in thousands to break even. In addition to scale, the manufacture of PCs required speed and flexibility that a closed economy did not provide (this was 1988, and the liberalization of the Indian economy was still some years away). Wipro needed someone who would become a conduit between the sales force in the field and the factory to help with burgeoning delivery issues. Basically, the job was sales coordination. The field reps had an all-time low confidence in the manufacturing division and the factory blamed the field reps for anything that went wrong. Given the chaotic situation, with an overworked army that did not enjoy anyone's respect, the job entailed some streamlining, and a lot of communication and influencing. I did not know the real dynamics between the players, and I did not care. I needed an organization that was stable and would give me a long-term career. It did not matter to me where I was placed in the organizational hierarchy. I have always believed that if you are good at your job, your position in the hierarchy does not matter in the long run.

On 1 March 1988 I arrived at Wipro's head office at 88 M.G. Road in Bangalore and reported to B.V. Venkatesh, vice president responsible for corporate sales. He in turn reported to Ashok Soota. My life as manager customer relations and sales support had begun; Wipro was going to be home for the next ten years of my life.

Joining a large organization with its own distinctive culture midway in the life of the organization is always fraught with uncertainty for any outsider. It requires an unusual amount of involvement by senior management to help the person succeed in the new environment. For high achievers, it is a matter of great risk. That is why you see many stars brought into an organization in positions of importance unable to perform after a while and no one quite knows why. A lot has been talked and written about the challenges of a new CEO coming to an organization. Yet, thousands of mid-level managers join new organizations routinely and go through a significant amount of struggle in making the transition work. In part, the incumbents bring the problem with themselves. When people make mid-career changes, I always hear them ask for a job that impacts corporate strategy, seeking a corner room with a large window, preferably close to the CEO, examining closely the organogram of the organization and hair-splitting on the exact nature of the job. No one says, 'Give me the challenge of a tough, dirty, and strategic role that no one is willing to take, something that may be keeping the CEO awake at night.' But when your outlook changes from 'What is good for me' to 'Where is the organization hurting and how can I make a difference', your professional landscape changes. A big reason why I quickly rooted into the new soil was the wholeheartedness with which I embraced the new job and accepted some of the changes that came along the way.

I was located at the head office in Bangalore. The real theatre of action was the factory at Mysore. As soon as my short assimilation at head office was over, I started travelling to Mysore, spending long days and nights at the factory. The sight and sound of the place took me back to my DCM days. Instead of cloth bales, here were computers. I saw first-hand the harried work life of the sales coordination manager and his dozen assistants. The key issue for me was to make the work of the sales coordination team transparent to the field organization, to create a collaborative culture between the field and the factory, improve responsiveness and help the team build pride in their work. Over a period of six months, I worked hand in hand with all of them, and things began to turn around. There was transparency and rich communication, and people felt confident enough that they broke the bad news first. The lowest man in the factory was empowered to make good short shipments and his performance was publicly recognized. The people who worked at the factory were sent to the field offices to see how the sales team worked and meet customers. I also made structural changes after a while and brought in new people, who then took charge. My work was a far cry from my erstwhile glamorous role in Project.21 that involved consulting with CEOs, evangelizing technology to an awestruck audience and being on the pages of *Dataquest* every month.

B.V. Venkatesh, my boss at Wipro, knew that I came from a training organization and that I missed that world. He suggested that I look after technical training, in addition to my transactional role in sales coordination. Ranjan Acharya, a highly competent manager, was already looking after that area. Neither Ranjan nor I were very sure of what value I could add. But as we started working together, we soon found a way for me to be useful. In addition, I had to handle all significant customer visits. In time, I started looking for additional opportunities in areas like leadership development and soon my hands were more than full. Or so I thought.

¤

Azim Premji, Wipro's chairman, walks with confidence and energy, exudes a certain restlessness and ambition, is disarmingly non-pretentious, extremely charismatic and quite a head-turner for his looks. One day, he suddenly appeared in my cubicle; he had apparently just dropped by to see how I was doing. The next thing I knew, we were closeted in a conference room for an hour discussing the worsening debtor situation the company faced. 'How loaded are you?' he asked me. I told him that 40 per cent of my time went into sales coordination, 40 per cent into training and 20 per cent into customer relations. 'Why don't you continue doing all that and spend an additional 20 per cent of your time on debtor management?' Premji rejoined. I told him that the math did not quite add up. To that, he replied, 'That is the precise point. Only when you are 120 per cent loaded will you be 100 per cent effective.' I took on debtor management.

At that time, Wipro's debtor problem was completely out of hand—receivables were never in line with the plan. But more than that, poor cash flow was hurting the company. Part of the problem was that the salesperson who had made the original sale had moved on, leaving behind orphaned accounts. Customers refused to pay, holding up huge amounts of money, sometimes citing minor short shipments as the reason. But at the bottom of it all, I realized, the biggest problem was the salespeople themselves: they were too shy to ask for money. The typical profile of the Wipro salesperson was a top-of-the-class engineer with a matching MBA. He was the most technically informed person in the whole industry.

He was also a 'decent guy', and good guys do not remind people if they are owed money. That was the mindset I needed to fix. Further, all bad receivables usually start with bad paperwork. A purchase order reveals the quality of the sales process behind it. In fact, on reading a purchase order I can diagnose the sales process and even predict what may happen downstream with receivables and customer satisfaction. Receivables and customer satisfaction always go hand in hand. A truly satisfied customer does not sit on your money. Salespeople and their bosses ignore vital signs in pursuit of a deal while chasing their quarterly numbers. They tend to think problems will solve themselves with the passage of time. Sometimes they do; usually problems not attended to just become bigger. Commitments on innocent-looking clauses such as supply of a non-standard peripheral that may be only 5 per cent of the total value of the invoice, linking the entire payment on delivery of that one peripheral, or agreeing to accept payment after uplinking has been completed in a place that is three days' away from head office—all these can delay payment, and are blind commitments made by salespeople wanting to make the sale.

Situations like this made me realize I needed to talk to the sales force. At a time when cash flow was so tight that all travel had been embargoed, I asked for a two-day conference and got all the area managers to fly in. The area managers were the ones who made the sales, but it was their bosses, the regional managers, who had so far interacted with head office. I had to break that mould and for the first time, during this conference, the head office spoke directly with the area managers on a critical issue. We discussed the cost of receivables, about how to read the signals that a customer could default on payments, and about the psychology behind not asking for money when it was due; we sought opinions, encouraged heated debates and took positions where necessary.

Azim Premji decided to drop by unannounced, pulled up a chair next to me and sat there for both days without uttering a word. His silence was eloquent. He sent the message that the issues being talked about had to be taken seriously and that I was in charge. After the conference, I travelled around the country, spoke to each salesperson in the field, introduced special incentives for them to collect receivables from orphaned accounts, stopped deliveries where past payments had not been received, forced errant customers to sit for negotiations where money had been held up for flimsy reasons, and trained the entire sales force on why it was okay to be an engineer with an MBA degree and still collect money like a small-town trader.

Finally, to build awareness and pride, I mounted a series of poster campaigns. One said 'Like Clean Water, Clean Orders are a Survival Issue'. Above the words was a beautiful picture of the Kaveri river; I had personally chosen the location for the photo shoot and overseen the production of the poster with the advertising agency. My brief to the agency was simple: create posters that were so good that people would like to take them home. We ran out of posters in no time. Interestingly, many of the customers demanded them and for the first time our coffers were full.

To me, it was all about winning a mind game. If I could make people understand the issues, they would take charge and deliver the results.

CHAPTER 12

The Journey Is the Reward

It is interesting how quickly seasons change in the corporate world. What was a priority yesterday may not be a priority today and your past glory is only as relevant as the current war.

My professional life at Wipro suddenly became uncertain when my boss B.V. Venkatesh decided to leave. His successor was unsure what to do with me. As luck would have it, I got hand-picked to work on a joint venture between Wipro and GE Medical Systems. I soon became part of a small team that helped get the joint venture, Wipro GE Medical Systems, off the ground and thereafter I became the marketing manager there. It took me into a different world altogether. I had never worked closely with a large multinational company. There was the additional complexity of integrating GE's sputtering India-based existing joint venture. Being in the middle of it all, I tried to love the people, the place and the products I was supposed to introduce into the market. However, somewhere deep inside me, I did not feel comfortable enough. I believe the reason is because temperamentally I am not suited to work in a joint venture: it entails being able to deal with a certain ambivalence and conflict of identity, and I am not comfortable with this. Most joint ventures are marriages of convenience; they can also just be an escort service and both sides are aware of that reality. Senior managers in a joint venture need to deal with surreal and sometimes very direct power plays. I am not particularly good at that sort of thing. Nor was I ready to settle down in a structured job as a middle-level manager that the Wipro GE position really required me to be. Having worked in a start-up like Project.21, I was unfit for a role that was largely implementational in nature. Fortunately for me, my journey was once again to take an unexpected turn.

This bend in my journey probably started when I had an argument with Ram Agarwal, a man three levels senior to me, within the first couple of months of joining Wipro's hardware business in 1988. Ram ran Wipro's printer business and was widely respected as an intrapreneur par excellence. The same factory that shipped computers also shipped printers to Original Equipment Manufacturers (OEMs). With tight production, there would be an occasional conflict between OEM and Wipro's captive needs. Ensuring supplies reached the

OEMs was Ram's responsibility. The manager in the factory who reported to me thus had to meet Ram's requirements as well. Once, Ram was very unhappy for some reason and shot off a very strong mail to the manager with copies to me and the factory's general manager. Around this very time, I was trying to boost my manager's flagging self-confidence and saw Ram's action as undoing my efforts. My understanding of the situation was that Ram should have spoken to me first about his misgivings before indicting one of my reportees. Ram had divergent views on the matter, and we argued about it for more than an hour one Saturday. Finally we ended the discussion by agreeing to disagree. I left his room concluding that the man would never speak to me again in his life.

Ram had subsequently moved out and taken charge of Wipro's international technology division. He and the executive vice president of R&D, Dr Sridhar Mitta, had sensed an opportunity to sell Wipro's R&D capabilities to companies in Silicon Valley. They needed a man on the ground there. The head of HR at Wipro, a burly, jovial man named Brian Jones, told them that the man they were looking for was in Wipro GE, but they could not recruit me. That would need Ashok Soota's advocacy with Azim Premji. And only Premji in turn could broach the matter with the GE management. Ram Agarwal was not a man to give up without trying. But first, he needed to speak with me.

The offer to go to the US to open an office from scratch to sell Wipro's R&D capability to companies like

Intel and Sun sounded so exhilarating that I was beside myself with joy when Ram told me the job could be mine. It took me no time to choose between staying on as marketing manager in Wipro GE and going to the US to start a ground-up operation that was fraught with uncertainty. The offer was of course subject to Azim Premji willing to talk to GE to release me.

After a few days of uncertainty, the issue was settled between Wipro and GE managements. I was free to go. I came home excited and informed Susmita. She had never travelled outside India and was saving money in a piggy bank to be able to go to Singapore on a vacation some day. And here I was telling her that we would be moving to the US! She could not believe her ears. Neha and Niti were eight and five then, so their education would not be affected. There was, however, one catch in all this. What would we do with my mother who lived with us? She had to be shifted to either Dadamoni's or Amitav's home. She did not like the idea of moving around because, due to her blindness, it meant readjusting each time she changed residence. We had shifted from Calcutta to Bangalore barely two years back and she was quite settled in her routine. It was a big price to pay, but an opportunity this huge did not come every other day. When we spoke to her, she wholeheartedly blessed the idea.

The assignment to start an operation in the US was just an idea in Ram Agarwal's and Dr Mitta's minds. Nothing existed on the ground—I was tasked with doing everything to make the idea a reality. Wipro needed permission from the Indian government to open an office in the US; there were immigration issues, tax matters and a whole host of other things that could stall the idea. We decided I needed to make a reconnaissance trip, spend a few weeks understanding what all was required and come back to get the Indian side of things moving.

¤

Dropping down from cruising altitude over the Pacific Ocean, lowering over the Napa Valley, and then making a final approach over the San Francisco Bay, the Singapore Airlines Boeing 747 aircraft landed in the afternoon sun and taxied on the runway with the gentleness of a giant. It was my maiden voyage to the land of opportunity. I had little idea of what lay ahead. I hardly knew anyone there, had no clue of how I was going to get started. When you embrace the uncertain, life opens up unusual new paths. Seeds sown way back bloom as flowers, in ways one can never fathom. As a writer for *Dataquest*, I had befriended Debasish Ghosh, a subeditor at the magazine. He had since migrated to the US. Now he volunteered to pick me up at the airport. As it was a reconnaissance trip, my family had not accompanied me. If all went to plan, I would be returning to India to bring them over.

Debasish drove me to the EZ8 Motel, where Wipro executives always stayed during their occasional visits to the Valley. At eighteen dollars a night, that was all the company could afford. It took me many months to

GO KISS THE WORLD

realize that it was not the best address in town because whenever someone asked me where I was staying, there was a fleetingly strange expression on their faces when I told them EZ8. I did not understand why that was so. Sometimes, ignorance is such a beautiful thing! For the next few days after my arrival, Debasish drove me around taking me from one meeting to another. He took me home, fed me, showed me the place inside out and finally added my name on his credit card so that I could become fully functional—he did everything to make me feel comfortable in an alien land.

I had two immediate tasks at hand. One, to meet with a group of Wipro R&D engineers who were stationed in the Valley working with Intel's R&D and, two, to meet a man named Atul Vijaykar at Intel who had godfathered the relationship between Wipro and Intel. Intel processors had become the de facto standard for the IBM PC. But Intel had not yet broken into the so-called 'glass house', that is, the formidable-looking corporate data centres that ran on servers and engineering workstations in environmentally controlled, high-security glass enclosures. For Intel, it was not only important to dominate the PC market but even more important to fend off workstation vendors and gain gradual entry into the server market. Wipro's R&D strengths could help Intel break into this market. Wipro engineers already worked as part of Intel teams; the engineers came and went on rotation for six months at a time. Wipro was allowed by the Reserve Bank of India to remit a measly sum of one thousand eight hundred dollars a month per engineer by way of 'maintenance allowance'. The engineers pooled their living expenses and on this tight budget lived slightly better than farm labour, illegal immigrants who came to pick the lettuce fields. These engineers toiled day and night to give Intel their best and, in turn, acquired knowledge that would help them design computers at home to keep Wipro in the lead. To these engineers, I was another 'management guy' who was not going to make any difference to their difficult living conditions. They viewed me with part cynicism, part hostility and certainly very low expectations. Among them were Namakkal Parthasarathy and Kalyan Banerjee who were to become co-founders of MindTree with me one day!

I knew I could not change their lot easily and certainly not overnight. Listening to all their woes the very first night over a shared meal in their apartment, I realized mobility was a big issue—not all of them had learnt to drive because of the meagre allowance. I returned to my motel and called the home office to 'inform' them that I had asked all engineers to take driving lessons and that the cost would be reimbursed. That one decision gave me their complete trust and became the transformational foundation of a self-confident R&D unit that eventually successfully repositioned itself into a global powerhouse over the next few years. Many small things followed—I took over the administrative chore of managing their pooled money, ran around to get them their licences and their apartments, picked them up from and dropped them to the airport, arranged for their families to join them, found schools for their children and stood by them during the occasional accident and hospital visit. The group of rag-tag soldiers suddenly saw a general in their midst, in the trenches, one who was willing to share their lot. It is amazing how a little empathy can be the starting point of larger things to come.

When I called on Atul Vijaykar, he greeted me with a welcome and a rebuke. On the one hand Atul was happy that Wipro had decided to step up its engagement in the Valley; on the other hand, he did not think Wipro was ambitious enough. He just did not see how Wipro could raise the bar for itself to aim to become at least a hundred million dollar company! He was there to help with the introductions and the little push to open doors, but would Wipro measure up? I told Atul that I would ensure that his message was delivered to the right people and I was there in all sincerity to make a difference. He was not sure how much to believe me but agreed to help nonetheless.

Not knowing anyone, I went about calling on people who at least had an India connection. While there were a bunch of Wipro engineers at the Intel labs, three others were learning chip design, thanks to a small entrepreneurial bet Dr Mitta and Ram Agarwal had placed. Wipro was a distributor of Sun Microsystems in India and Dr Mitta and Ram had agreed to loan three Sun workstations to a start-up led by three Indians. They used to work at VLSI Technologies. In return for the use of the Sun workstations, they had agreed that three

Wipro hardware designers could train on a few of VLSI's chip-design tools in California. I met Tushar Dave, the man behind this deal, who became a venture capitalist in later years. I also met the people who had started the Silicon Valley Indian Professionals Association (SIPA) and a few others to see how Wipro could get a foothold in the Valley and start a larger operation. I met with existing larger players like HCL America and TCS and many others to understand issues on the ground. Finally, I called on a father–son duo who used to rent cars to our engineers without insisting on credit cards or insurance. To me, they were important stakeholders of my success and when Susmita arrived, they were the first to be called home for a meal.

After sizing up the realities on the ground and the opportunities ahead, I returned to India to submit a feasibility report to the Reserve Bank of India to open a branch office for Wipro in California. This was part of a mandatory process after which the Reserve Bank would allow a company to buy the foreign exchange needed to spend overseas. The Reserve Bank had total control and rationed foreign exchange because India did not have enough reserves. We put together a business plan that sought twenty thousand dollars as a one-time expense to open the office and another twelve thousand dollars a month as recurring expenses. Armed with the plan, I went to the Reserve Bank of India's Mumbai office and pleaded our case. An officer offered all of ten thousand dollars for the first year and declined to help beyond that. How could Wipro be given foreign exchange when it had no track record of earning through exports, was his contention. The law allowed only a certain percentage of all export earnings to be used for opening branch offices and associated marketing activities. The impossibility of enhancing export earnings without first opening an office did not make sense to the custodians of the economy because India's foreign exchange situation had always been hand to mouth. Disheartened, I returned to Bangalore. Dr Mitta, Ram Agarwal and I agreed that we would drop the idea of setting up a proper office for now. Instead I would go back as a business visitor and would begin operations from a home office, hustle for projects, earn some money and then go back to the Reserve Bank once Wipro's export earnings had improved.

¤

I returned to the US with Susmita and our two girls in August 1991. We found an apartment in Cupertino in about a week's time. Neha and Niti were admitted into a public school in a good school district. I purchased a hundred and ten dollar Brother electronic typewriter and a fax machine with the help of Debasish Ghosh. Back home in India, in Wipro's head office, only the president had a fax machine! I set up the typewriter and fax machine next to the dining table, and with that Wipro was open for business in the Valley. I tried to sweet talk Susmita into picking up the phone when it rang with the suggested greeting, 'Wipro, good morning. How may I help you?' She put her foot down and let me know that it wasn't part of the deal when she had agreed to follow me to the other end of the world. Shrugging off the setback, I started in right earnest.

Having a home office is not the easiest way to run a business. When the two girls would return from school in the afternoon, they would grab the television remote and sit glued in front of it, watching Scooby Doo or Yogi Bear, with the volume loud enough to let a caller know this was no regular office. So, I entered into a pact with them. If the phone rang while they were watching television, they had to dash for the remote and mute the television within the proverbial two rings. Then, with a brisk, 'Good afternoon, this is Subroto Bagchi', I would begin my business conversation. The girls cooperated most of the time—except when they sat on the remote and forgot where to look for it or it slid between two cushions. The arrangement worked well enough without major problems, other than the fact that I could not have business meetings in my so-called office. I met customers over breakfast or lunch in restaurants so that people would not know that Wipro did not even have an office worth the name.

The whole pretence gave way when one day I received a call from Som Das, at that time a director at VLSI at San Jose. He was a founder-member of SIPA and was calling to see how he could help me. Som wanted to come over to meet me in my office. I tried to fix a breakfast or lunch meeting, and even offered to come up to meet him in his office. He would not agree. As Som was free only after nine at night he suggested he would drop by on his way home. After all, he had a day job and helping out fledgling Indian companies was just an altruistic, after-hours activity for him. Cornered, I blurted out that I actually operated out of home. Surprisingly, it did not matter to him.

Som Das arrived just past nine one night and we kept talking in my sparsely furnished drawing room till close to midnight, discussing how he could help me. The direct fallout of the meeting was an introduction to a man named Kris Narayan who was running the VLSI chipset design team on a project for Apple. Following this, Kris and I met for breakfast. Kris needed board designers and I needed more Wipro engineers to learn VLSI design. We started working closely. The relationship grew from strength to strength. When Kris moved on we developed a relationship with his boss Umesh Paudwal. When Umesh started his own company, Wipro forged a relationship with that company. Soon that start-up was bought out by Cisco and Cisco in turn became Wipro's customer.

Thus, the unselfish help of people like Debasish Ghosh, Atul Vijaykar, Som Das and countless others was instrumental in establishing a completely unknown company. Neither I nor they knew that one day Wipro would become a household name in Silicon Valley. The journey was indeed the reward.

In the course of the journey, many fortuitous things happened. One such was a relationship with Tandem. Wipro represented Tandem in India to sell their range of fault-tolerant computers, and Tandem used Wipro engineers for some of its operating systems work. Tandem used a proprietary operating system called Guardian, which was a closely guarded technology. A chance meeting with Sath Sathyanarayan who worked with Tandem at a talk organized by SIPA led to Wipro participating in Tandem's international R&D programme; Wipro engineers began to learn Guardian. In a couple of months, Wipro's Bangalore office had the largest Tandem installation in the Asia-Pacific worth many millions of dollars, loaned by Tandem in perpetuity. Eventually Wipro's Bangalore office became the only place in the world with Guardian expertise as Tandem's own R&D was phased out due to a takeover. Tandem's fault-tolerant computers ran stock exchange applications, 9-1-1 emergency numbers and the assembly lines of Mercedes Benz. A time came when any trouble with these computers meant that only a Wipro engineer could fly down and fix it. Wipro's business grew from strength to strength.

¤

The relationship with Intel, VLSI and Tandem gave Wipro a strong footing. Word got around that Wipro was good. Yet, none of us were the kind to rest on our laurels. We planned on building a globally admired lab-on-hire. Ashok Soota, president of Wipro, would not be satisfied till we had acquired Sun Microsystems as a client. After all, Wipro represented Sun Microsystems in India, so why couldn't they use Wipro's R&D capabilities?

Walt Brown, an athletic and handsome ham radio enthusiast, who used to be the top man for Sun Microsystems in Singapore and knew Ashok returned to the Valley to manage the support operations at Sunsoft, Sun's newly spun-off software outfit. He had no use for us but liked Ashok too much to say that. He suggested that I meet his assistant Tom Best, an ex-IBM engineer.

A few days later, armed with a briefcase that I still cherish, I knocked on Tom's office door. A man in his fifties, he reminded me of a friendly seal off the Pacific Coast; I do not know why. As soon as we exchanged greetings, he said, 'I do not even know where India is.' Without losing my presence of mind, I dropped my briefcase on the floor next to his desk, picked up a marker pen and in silence for the next few minutes focussed on drawing a world map on his white board. All the while, I was aware of a pair of fascinated eyes following my hand as the map evolved.

As a child, father had initiated me into drawing maps and created in me affection for geography. His younger brother had risen to become a professor of geography at the prestigious Calcutta University. He was also a nationalist who had joined Gandhi during the historic walk to riot-torn Noakhali along with Frontier Gandhi, Khan Abdul Ghaffar Khan. We were raised with my uncle as a benchmark. And here I was, in Tom's office, reliving the map-drawing experiences of my childhood, hopefully making Professor Kanan Gopal Bagchi, my uncle, proud.

As I was detailing Asia, Tom broke the silence: 'I know where Singapore is,' he said. I turned back, smiled and showed him where India was vis-à-vis Singapore. Tom looked at the white board and exclaimed, 'You draw a world map rather well.' Tom did not grill me on technology. It did not matter to him. He liked what he had seen. Along with another colleague named Bob Beaulieu, Tom was about to set up an R&D unit to help software designers all over the world write applications on Sun's own version of UNIX, called Solaris. Bob and he had the charter but not much else. We agreed that two Wipro R&D engineers, Bharat Suraiya and Sunil Kand, would be their handymen. From an undefined, nebulous and small relationship, things started moving. In time, we created a large, multi-year deal with Sun to set up an R&D support centre code-named Orbit 1.

Things had just started to take-off at Sun when Tom called to inform me he was moving on to Salt Lake City. He had had enough of the burn and churn of the Valley. He wanted to move to the mountains. Novell was offering him a job as head of support. Salt Lake City was a place where he could ski his way to retirement. Thanks to a great relationship Bharat Suraiya had established with Bob, business boomed despite Tom's absence.

We were now earning enough to move the home office to a two-roomed rental in a business district. The only problem was that I was the lone occupant of that office; occasionally Susmita would drive by to leave me a flask of home-made tea. I kept the old typewriter on a desk near the front door so that people would think there was a receptionist who had just stepped out. In reality, it did not matter because I never had meetings in office and the FedEx and UPS delivery guys knew very well that this was a one-man operation. Looking back, the big-company pretence was important for my own benefit. It kept me going. We formally inaugurated the office on Ashok's next visit along with the engineers, their spouses and children.

There were more than a hundred engineers now. Days were busy with multiple clients. People lived well and their families could join them for long-term stay. We ran a proper payroll, paid taxes in the US, and set up regular health insurance plans. Susmita would help the new families settle in—showing them the elementary schools, the Indian grocery stores, the inoculation centres and the county libraries, and helping them take their driving test at the Department of Motor Vehicles.

One of the challenges of setting up an R&D operation in the US was the complete lack of cross-cultural understanding on the part of the engineers. I approached the University of California's Santa Cruz Extension Centre to check if they could custom design a training course for us. Lu-Ellen Schaffer was given the charter by the university to create the course design. Thereafter, she started her own organization and over the next two decades, she consulted with thousands of Indians and Americans on how to work together. Today, she is a very good friend and has become a member of the Bagchi family.

¤

March 1992. We had spent an entire day at the park with the children—Lu-Ellen had invited us for an Easter egg hunt and a family picnic. The day had been perfect, and we returned home late in the afternoon, tired and happy. The phone was ringing as we entered.

It was Dadamoni from India. Father, who was now eighty-one, staying with Dadamoni in New Delhi, had been hospitalized. Father had over the years developed a cataract and his vision had deteriorated. But he was nervous about getting it operated and we had all agreed not to force him. He had irregular sleep, frequently woke up at night, and smoked a cigarette before trying to sleep again. The night before, he had woken up at about 2 a.m. and while lighting a matchstick, accidentally, his clothes had caught fire. Groggy with the after-effects of years of psychotropic drugs, he failed to handle the fire or call for help. When the fire spread, it was mother who sensed the heat and intuitively realized what had happened. She raised an alarm. By the time Dadamoni could rush in from his bedroom at the far end of the house, father had collapsed on the floor with third-degree burns. He was admitted to Safdarjang Hospital. The doctors had advised Dadamoni that all the other children be called—only a miracle could now save him and it was apparent that time was running out.

I wanted to cry but that was not part of the training he had imparted. I took the first available flight and was driven straight to the hospital on my arrival in Delhi. As I stood by his bedside, he looked at me, no remorse, no self-pity, just muted, subdued pain. I sat there for a long while and then moved to find a place on the portico steps as the clouds broke overhead.

A burn ward is a very difficult place, and in a government hospital like Safdarjang Hospital the resources are stretched and the hospital staff overworked. One morning, while attending to my father, I realized that the intravenous fluid bottle was empty and fearing that air would go into his vein, I asked the attending nurse to change it. She bluntly told me to do it myself. In the horrible theatre of death of a burn ward, I was in pain and frustration and anger. Finally when she relented and came, my father opened his eyes and murmured to her, 'Why have you not gone home yet?' Here was a man on his deathbed but more concerned about an overworked nurse than his own state of pain. I was stunned. From him I learnt that there is no limit to how concerned you can be for another human being and the limit of inclusion you draw. My father died the next day.

After the usual formalities surrounding cases of death by injury, we brought his body home. My mother was stoic in her response. She touched his feet in silence as one last gesture of respect. 'Can we take him now?' I asked her. From the corners of her eyes, sunken deep with the lack of vision, she wiped a teardrop and murmured, 'Yes.' We took him to the crematorium. For his final journey, a packet of the best Darjeeling tea and his preferred brand of cigarettes were kept alongside him as the metal cover separating the mortal world and the all-engulfing flames of the electric furnace opened and closed.

Next day, I went back to San Francisco.

CHAPTER 13

What Is Success?

As a four-year-old, I would often ask my father what work he actually did. Every time, he would explain to me with gentle pride that he was a judicial magistrate.

'What does a judicial magistrate do, Baba?'

'He puts people who do wrong things on trial.'

'Buldul pinched me today with his big fat toe, Baba. Put him on trial.'

'Okay, I'll put him on trial. First, you must write down a list of all the wrong things he does.'

'Baba, put Ma on trial also.'

'Now, what has she done?'

That afternoon, I had witnessed a group of tribal men and women dancing down the road in merry abandon. At some distance, a flower-bedecked couple followed them. I went running to my mother to ask her what the occasion was. She told me that the young couple had just got married and the bride was being taken to the groom's village. Married? What was that? I was completely perplexed. 'Everyone gets married,' she tried to explain. I was still quite confused and asked her haltingly, 'Are you married?' She was amused.

'Yes, to your father.'

I was very annoyed with her for that reply because I thought marriage was an inappropriate thing to do for I had just seen inebriated folk making merry on the road.

So, right this moment, I was asking the judicial magistrate to put her on trial as well.

¤

I was his Chhote Lal; that's what my father used to call me as a little boy. He would often talk to me in Hindi so that I could learn the language well. 'Jawaharlal Nehru says it is the national language and you must learn to speak it well,' he would exhort us. Despite his small-time government job in remote and inaccessible areas, he was always tuned in to Nehru's priorities! Every day, after returning from work, he would have his evening cup of tea and walk to the district officers' club. For most officers, it was a place for bridge and some bureaucratic gossip. My father would head straight to an oversize transistor radio that sat on a large table to catch the seven o'clock BBC news bulletin. Then he would return home to tell us the news of the world as we sat on the floor for dinner as a family. Thus, even as a small boy, in places as far away as Koraput and Keonjhar, I was aware of the détente and entente during the cold war, Kissinger's ping-pong diplomacy and realpolitik, Lyndon Johnson and Harold Wilson, U. Thant and Menachem Begin, Moshe Dayan and Leonid Brezhnev—it seemed as if these globetrotting statesmen were family friends who visited us with astounding regularity.

Father was extremely gentle with me during the very few transgressions in my childhood. In Koraput, after his first cup of tea every morning, he would sit on the veranda cross-legged, place a small mirror at a short distance, take out his shaving kit and with a mug of water by his side work up a rich lather from a shaving cup, thereby beginning a ceremoniously long shave. During the entire time, as he first foamed his face, then carefully shaved with a razor blade and repeated the sequence one more time, Aurobinda and I would dutifully take out our handwriting books and readers and study under his tutelage. His attention would alternate between us. After the ritual, Aurobinda would get ready to go to school and father to office. I was then by myself for most of the day until my brother would return in the afternoon.

During those long days, I made friends with Ram Das, a man who occasionally came home to help mother with odd jobs. He used to smoke beedis. One afternoon, he was intently doing something with his half-smoked beedi resting on the window sill. In my playfulness, I grabbed it and took a puff. He was aghast. His shock was not because I, barely five years old, had smoked, but because I had smoked his used beedi. He chastised me, 'Babu, why are you doing that? You could always ask for a fresh one.' That was a bonanza. For the next few days, I got a beedi every day from Ram Das and it was our little secret. I felt very proud of my achievement.

The following Saturday, Aurobinda came home early from school. He had stolen a tomato from mother's kitchen. In a place like Koraput, it was a precious vegetable. Brimming with the satisfaction of a job well executed, Aurobinda took out the bright red tomato from his pocket and showed it off to me. I wanted to show him I was no less of an achiever and took out that day's gift from Ram Das to demonstrate my one-upmanship. His face froze.

The next day, after both of us had fought over some issue, he promptly told my father about the beedis I used to get from Ram Das. I thought the world had come to an end. Though father seldom physically punished us— I recall being slapped only once—we were reasonably respectful of his displeasure. And here I was, with a serious enough charge that justified hanging me upside down. Father heard Aurobinda out and said nothing. He knew very well that I had crossed the line. He did not utter a word. I protested loudly; my total lack of conviction struck a hollow note even to my own ears. I fell quiet. The few seconds of silence felt like aeons. Then he said, without looking at us, 'If that is what he wants, I will send him away to an ashram school and he can smoke there as much as he likes.' With that pronouncement, court was adjourned. Ashram schools were residential schools run by the government for tribal children.

Father did not bring up the subject with me ever again. I could not look him in the face for many days. Sometimes, not handing out the punishment when it is most expected is the best way to bring lasting repentance.

¤

One of the signs of prosperity in a small town was the transistor radio and many of our friends had one in their homes. Whenever I would show my father advertisements for Philips, Murphy and Bush radio sets in the newspapers and ask him when he would buy one, he would reply that he already had five sets and did not need one more.

I would see my friends living in their own houses.

'When will you buy a house?' I would often ask father.

'I already have five houses, why do I need one more?' he would reply.

The five houses and five radio sets were his five sons. Material success did not define my father. He was a man whose success was defined by his principles, his frugality and his universalism. Above all, he taught me that success is your ability to rise above your discomfort, whatever be your current state of wealth. You can, if you want, raise your consciousness above your immediate surroundings. Success is not about building material comforts—the transistor radio that he could never buy or the house that he never owned. His success was the legacy he left, the memetic continuity of his ideals that grew beyond the smallness of an ill-paid, unrecognized government servant's world.

CHAPTER 14

Learning to Listen

Three years of hard work in the Valley had borne fruit. Things were on an upward trajectory. Ever since my father's death, I had wanted to come back to India. Among my reasons was the desire to bring my mother back to stay with us. I requested Dr Mitta to bring me back to Bangalore. Though he would have liked me to continue in the US for some more time, he understood my feelings. We returned in 1993.

Most people covet good jobs, great postings, higher salaries than their friends and a rather elusive elixir called job satisfaction. Conceding that all these are legitimate desires for every professional, I would, however, trade all of that for the opportunity to work for a great boss. To get just a couple of them in an entire career, one has to work really hard and be lucky at the same time. I was lucky to work under one such man who allowed me to grow to become the first chief executive of Wipro's global R&D.

Born in 1947, Dr Sridhar Mitta came from a well-to-do, conservative trading family in Chittoor, near Tirupati, in Andhra Pradesh. He was expected to join the family business of prescription medicine. One of his teachers in high school decided his fate when he decreed that instead of studying commerce, young Sridhar had to study mathematics and science so that he could become an engineer. From that point onwards, his family did not quite understand what he was doing. After completing his master's at IIT, he went off to the US where he earned his doctorate and returned to India to work where the geniuses of his generation worked: the Bhabha Atomic Research Centre. He moved to the Electronic Corporation of India Limited, a government-owned company, that made 16- and 32-bit computers, electronic store and forward machines and a variety of control systems for India's space and defence needs. He was the first man Azim Premji hired when he and his chief finance officer, Ashok Narasimhan, decided to move into the computer business sometime in 1981. Dr Mitta set up Wipro's R&D from scratch.

In the 1990s, Wipro came to be highly respected for its indigenous R&D that designed hardware and ported operating systems, implemented network protocols and wrote device drivers. It consisted of eighty highly competent engineers. They were Dr Mitta's children. In the R&D division, he was referred to as god. The reason was simple—he had time for all creation, big and small, and like god, he knew the answer to every question. He was friend, philosopher, guide to everyone and people knew that he was the man in charge. For a man of his position, physically one would consider him nondescript till he touched you in some way.

¤

From Dr Mitta I learnt that the first rule for managing is to listen. This is something most bosses find difficult to do because they do not know that in order to listen, you must first suspend all judgement. As chief technology officer of the corporation, Dr Mitta was an epitome of accessibility. The juniormost engineer could simply walk into his office, pull up a chair and sound out what could sometimes be the most absurd technical idea or a trivial personal issue. Dr Mitta would always first listen intently, before offering his advice.

He also taught me the meaning of humility, that knowledge and arrogance are antithetical. To be a good leader, one must first be a good human being.

R&D engineers can often do bizarre things—put the wrong end of the connector into the socket of the only working prototype board, drive a rented car into a stationary object in the middle of a deserted road in a foreign country or mix up the flight number on the ticket with the gate number, thereby missing a flight altogether. From Dr Mitta I learnt the key was not to react to what had happened. Whatever the incident, you had to learn to absorb all the details and then figure out subsequent damage control. In fact, Dr Mitta was almost Zen-like in his approach in this regard.

My challenge on my return to India was to give Wipro's R&D offices a contemporary look. For all its years of existence, Wipro had been a frugal corporation. As I went about my job, managers from other divisions developed a feeling that I was not cost conscious and this was reflected in my 360-degree feedback. This upset me greatly and I went to see Dr Mitta about it. In his characteristic style, he heard me out. Then he told me that we live in a world in which perception is reality. And that it takes time for perception to build up. So, the solution for me was to go back and do my work but be aware of my actions and what I said.

I took his advice to heart, and did all that he had advised with care. Next year, I received the same feedback from some peers. This time I was devastated. Once again I expressed my frustration to Dr Mitta. As usual he listened to me patiently and then told me, 'While it takes time to build perceptions, it takes *even longer* for perceptions to change.' I was dumbfounded by this statement. Realizing how true the statement was, I went back to my office and focussed on doing the right things the right way. In our work, we need to be sensitive to feedback and work to correct ourselves but we should not expect people to change what they think of us overnight. This should not cause us to lose spirit— negative public opinion most often has some basis and we must have the grace to accept it.

Under Dr Mitta's sage guidance, I flourished; over a period of five years, the transformation of the R&D division was complete and amazing. It largely had to do with the intrinsic quality of the people who constituted the division and Dr Mitta's leadership. From an inward-looking cost centre, it became a solidly profitable lab-on-hire.

CHAPTER 15

Who Is a Good Leader?

India had changed. I realized this when I returned in 1993, after my first stint in the US. The market had opened up and every day a new multinational started shop; incredible jobs were on offer. I was blown away by an offer from an aircraft engine company that offered me nine times the salary I was drawing at Wipro. I could retire at forty, I told myself, a stupid goal a lot of young people set for themselves at a certain phase in life. When I told Dr Mitta I had decided to leave, he was very sad. After a long conversation with me, he asked me to go and see Ashok the next day.

The following morning as I sat in Ashok's drawing room, I mentally went over the well-rehearsed set of answers I had prepared to every question I thought he could possibly ask. I envisaged he would sweet talk me into staying; after all, I was a star performer. Ashok walked in, shook hands and as we sat down, told me in a very matter-of-fact tone that I was getting enticed by a 'stupid job'. My jaw fell. Here I was with a job offer to earn a salary higher than Ashok's, and he had said I had landed a stupid job! Was he implying that I was stupid enough to have landed a stupid job? When Ashok was done, I realized that there had to be some truth in what he was saying. I was indeed trying to be someone I was not cut out to be. I was an IT industry person who made a living by selling software services. The world of aircraft engines involved dynamics that I had no clue about. Eventually, after some more reflection, I decided to stay back at Wipro. Half the time I see leaders pussy-foot around issues, seeking compromises which are unnecessary and saying things they do not mean. But that was not Ashok—he had given me the cold, hard truth about myself.

Ashok Soota is an interesting leader from many different standpoints. An electrical engineer from Roorkee, he started his life at Burmah Shell in the 1960s and quickly moved from there to become a senior management trainee at DCM. He went on to head Usha Fans and then took over Shriram Refrigeration. He then completed his MBA at the Asian Institute of Management at Manila to eventually become president of Wipro's IT business. When he took over the reins at Wipro, the turnover was two million dollars; when he left to co-found MindTree, Wipro's IT business had grown to five hundred million dollars.

Ashok never had the opportunity to handpick the team he worked with. At Shriram, he inherited the business and its structure. At Wipro, he inherited a top team that was already in place. At MindTree, out of the ten of us, he was the ninth co-founder and by the time he came on board we had already progressed on many key issues. Out of the eight co-founders already on board, Ashok did not even know four of them.

Despite this, he has always delivered results guided by a personal conviction that there are no 'A' teams and 'B' teams—there are only different types of leaders who make the teams the way they are. As a result, in every organization, he has always delivered extraordinary results with ordinary people.

Ashok is a champion of diversity. Working with him I learnt to respect people, to prize them for what they can do, not for what they have already done.

Ashok has no ego—he carries his own bag, stays in fifty-dollars-a-day hotels when travelling abroad, always insists everyone call him by his first name, replies to any email within twenty-four hours, paying the same level of attention whether the mail is from the juniormost employee or a Fortune 500 client.

Leadership is about personal character. It is important for any leader to have the highest sense of fairness in personal and professional dealings. A man like Ashok does not need to cultivate followers; they simply go with him because they know he has character. Anyone who has sat with Ashok at the negotiating table has never left with the feeling that he has been talked into an unfair deal.

Sometimes, in times of crisis, managers psych themselves into believing that doomsday is near. They come and tell their leaders why a decision has to be taken based only on the recommendations they have made. 'If we do not release this ad *today*, we will lose to the competition', 'If we do not revise salaries *now*, we will not get anybody to join us', 'If we do not agree to his terms, he *will* take us to court': leaders are often rushed into decisions on hearing such statements.

Ashok taught me a leader must not take decisions under such fraught circumstances. Always insist on some more time so that you can take a considered view, stepping away from the moment of high emotion. No decision is without risk, but when you take the time to think things through, you take very few regrettable decisions.

The importance of data when taking decisions cannot be underemphasized. Ashok epitomizes the rational and the deeply intuitive. He uses the power of intuition to look for opportunities, create alliances and, sometimes, to gauge an adversary's moves. But while taking decisions he never uses his intuition without the touchstone of data; and whenever he is smothered with data, he questions it with his intuition.

But the most important lesson I learnt from him was that all battles should be based on principles. And in a battle based on principles, it is not the size of the adversary that matters. It is the size of the principle. Time and again I have seen him coping with powerful opponents who have had the capability to inflict significant damage. In each instance, Ashok continued fighting on the strength of his principles. And in most cases, the man prevailed.

CHAPTER 16

The Entrepreneur as Leader

The pinnacle of my career at Wipro brought with it the opportunity to work directly for Azim Premji. Dr Mitta had taught me to be a good human being before trying to be a leader. From Ashok Soota I learnt what it takes to be a good leader. It was by observing Azim Premji at close quarters that I learnt about leadership from an entrepreneurial standpoint.

Azim Premji always had great admiration for GE as a company and Jack Welch as a leader. He saw tremendous similarities between GE and Wipro, though they differed vastly in scale. Both companies had diversified businesses, dealt with the basic and the hi-tech with the same ease and had great regard for values, systems, processes and leadership development. Azim

Premji's introduction to Jack Welch was preceded by his acquaintance with Larry Bossidy, an ex-GE executive who was chairman of Allied Signal. Larry was a great fan of Six Sigma and he had introduced the concept to Jack Welch. Azim Premji saw GE as a bell-weather company. He was also acutely aware of the challenges that lay ahead for Indian companies in a progressively open economy. Not only did product quality have to improve, process quality and attendant management styles would require transformation. Like Welch, he saw quality as a transformational agent. He also saw it as the common language that would unify his five disparate businesses.

In April 1996 I was appointed to Premji's office as his corporate vice president Mission: Quality. I now interacted with Azim Premji very frequently. It took me a while to lose my awe of him. Today I realize that managers who work for very senior people must not remain in awe of their bosses if they are to be effective. But it was a while before I could treat Premji as an equal.

As I had no previous experience in Quality, I was interested to know why I had been chosen for the job and not an expert in that field. When I asked, Premji said it was because he wanted someone with a 'sense of history'. At that time, I didn't completely understand what he meant.

Sense of history—such a beautiful, powerful, uplifting thought! Many of us excel as first-rate line managers. Then comes an assignment that calls not just for functional expertise; it requires the capability to make an impact without necessarily having the authority. Such assignments require bringing about change in people's ways of doing things; to achieve this you need someone who has a sense of history. Only such a person understands the existential issues, the challenges, and the larger purpose for the changes being made. These are individuals who create a vision for their people and move them out of their zone of comfort to try new things. Only those who have a sense of history can create a future. This, as a key job requirement, is seldom understood by people who choose staff for assignments that need large-scale change management.

Premji wanted me to produce a road map for change within days of taking charge. I was at sea because I felt I needed to understand the concept of Quality before coming up with a road map. Every week he would call and ask if the road map was ready. Each time I would repeat the same story: that I would like to understand from other companies how they had done it, read books, meet consultants in the field, get my own feel and only then come up with a road map. I could not predict how much time all this would take and he could not wait. When Premji pushed me too hard I lost my cool one day and told him that either he wait for me to create the road map my way or, if he already knew it himself, he could simply give it to me so that I could run with it. He remained unruffled and said, 'My job is to push you till you find your own limit. When you do, you have to push back. I do not have the road map. You have to create one on your own.' He went on to tell me that the most successful US presidents were those who knew what they wanted to do and how to go about it within the first ninety days in office. This fact applies to all senior-level jobs as well. If you cannot put down what you want to achieve within the first ninety days, you are probably never going to get anything done.

I started my quest. I read up volumes on the subject. I visited companies in India. I went to Japan. I visited GE's units in New York and Cincinnati and went to Texas Instruments in Dallas and to Motorola in Chicago. Finally, after studying alternative approaches, I presented two options to Wipro's chief executive council. The council chose to adopt Six Sigma as the framework for Wipro's journey to Quality and we began to roll out a sustained initiative over a prolonged period through leadership development, capacity creation at team levels and adoption of pilot projects. Yet, for me, it was a frustrating experience in some ways. Azim Premji ran his businesses through four presidents: Ashok Soota who looked after IT, P.S. Pai who looked after consumer products, M.S. Rao who looked after the fluid power business and S.R. Gopalan who looked after the group's financial services business (which does not exist any more). Despite Wipro being largely owned by Premji, he never treated his presidents as anything but equals. While he would create the urgency, he would not run any initiative with a fiat. As a result, the extent of adoption of change that Six Sigma entailed varied from division to division. When I used to get frustrated with the slow and uneven pace of change, he maintained equanimity because he held the longer-term view.

From Premji, I learnt the power of simplicity and forthrightness. His simplicity comes out in the way he writes, the way he speaks and dresses, what he eats and the way he addresses issues. You never have to wonder what is on his mind, for he speaks his mind. Adopting simplicity in thinking, communication and strategy is often the most difficult task. Before anything else, it requires people to be comfortable with who they are. Many managers think that overtly simple things are not impressive enough. But the more we complicate the message, the more difficult it becomes for people to understand it. Lesser the understanding by the team, higher is the inability to follow the leader.

A great leader has the capability to attract and retain talent that is better than him in many aspects. He does not get insecure when surrounding himself with a top performing team. Yet, the better the team, the higher the incidence of idiosyncrasy among team members.

At Wipro there was a very senior manager who often used to openly and virulently criticize Premji. He would even do this in front of Premji. But Premji never used to get ruffled by it. One day, I asked Premji why he put up with such behaviour. He calmly replied that this man consistently delivered on his commitments. Leaders must be comfortable with idiosyncratic people. Many high performers have their own quirks.

A leader's job is to focus on what is delivered, not on what a person's quirks are. Competence to do a job has far greater weightage than personal reverence.

Azim Premji is a brilliant strategist. All strategy to him begins with questioning the state of things even when everything is going well. Success always creates entrapment; it is much easier to stay with the familiar.

When it comes to matters of integrity, Premji looks at issues in black and white. For him, there are no shades of grey. When the average Wipro employee goes home at night, he sleeps well because the system does not expect him to do anything unethical to source or execute business. In fact, he can walk out of a negotiation if it is contingent upon any underhand dealings.

But I learnt my final lesson on leadership from Premji on my last day at Wipro. He wanted me to stay back. I told him that one of my reasons for leaving was that we were very different people, we thought differently. He answered: '*That* is the reason we should work together.'

When we look to hire people, we invariably look for sameness. It is so much more comfortable. But progress requires intelligent friction, push back, points and healthy counterpoints. The job of leaders is to build high personal comfort with contrarians who think differently, create alternative points of view and have the power to question the state of things.

CHAPTER 17

Coping with Mid-life Crisis

If we consider a thirty-year career span for most professionals, the years between the ages of twenty and thirty can be considered the years of self-discovery. The succeeding ten years are years of self-confidence and the forties are usually years of self-doubt. As a professional, you will find that at twenty you are bubbly, raring to go. Joining any organization at an entry-level position, you work your way through three or four different roles and eventually begin to settle down. You use those years to discover your own likes and dislikes.

Between the years of thirty and forty, once you've built a strong professional foundation, anything that you touch seems to turn to gold. You are confident that any assignment you are given will be a success. You never question your ability to add value to the assignment, the team and the organization.

Then one day you turn forty and self-doubt begins to emerge. What am I value-adding? Am I value-adding at all? Is all that I'm doing really worth the effort? Where am I going? What next for me? How well have I really done professionally, monetarily and in terms of organizational recognition vis-à-vis my batch mates? Where is my work–life balance? These not-so-unique questions—some real, some imagined—begin haunting you. Those who are lucky work their way out of such self-doubt fairly easily and on their own; some get bogged down and mired in the self-doubt. One common reason for this is the lack of sounding boards and support systems to help with the answers. Most suffer in silence. Many do not realize that they are making not just a professional transition but a mid-life transition. In an acute form, it is called the mid-life crisis.

Dr Elliot Jacques first coined the term mid-life crisis in 1965 in a study of creative geniuses. He found that during this period there are abrupt changes in lifestyle or productivity. It is accompanied by a desire for change brought on by fears and anxieties about growing old. In the IT industry in particular, the chances of an accelerated onset of mid-life crisis are probably much higher. For a high achiever, it could begin as early as thirty-five.

Studies indicate that there are two major periods of transition for all of us in life. The first one is the period of adolescence. It is meant to transform you from a child to an adult. A lot less is known or talked about the transition from adulthood to mid-life. Experts say this second period of transition is meant to move you to some place positive, essentially guiding you to psychological and spiritual completeness. Yet, it begins with a heightened sense of incompleteness, a pronounced sense of loss and inadequacy. For IT industry professionals, sometimes it brings a triple whammy. To begin with, there is a mid-life transition. Then there is the transition from middle management to senior management. The third jolt marks a time of accelerated obsolescence as learning slows down and much younger people demonstrate far greater skills.

Dr Andrew Leuchter, a noted authority on the subject, says, 'When people are in their twenties and thirties, a number of different career or personal paths are open. When they get into their forties, they begin to realize that they have made decisions that are either irrevocable or can be changed only with great difficulty. It is also a time when they begin to recognize that they have physical limitations.'

One of the most common signs is discontent with life or the very same lifestyle that gave you happiness for many years. There is a sense of boredom with people who hitherto held your interest or dominated your life. These could be close friends, professional associates, a role model or relatives at home. Some people feel highly adventurous and want to do something completely different. I know of people who never found time to play a sport in all their life suddenly wanting to go bungee jumping or para-sailing. Wall Street traders run away from their jobs and pay money to live in a ranch and herd cattle. Some people question the very meaning of life and the validity of past decisions.

In all this, there is confusion about who they are and where they are going. The most common outcome of this acute period of transition is a job change. In a personal sense, this is also a period marked for some with a high traction towards an extra-marital affair or a divorce. While the period of mid-life transition is as inevitable as adolescence, there are things one can do to manage it better and make it less fraught with reactive decisions that can have very difficult consequences.

¤

I turned forty in May 1997. I was at the height of my professional career at Wipro; I was the youngest among Premji's direct reports. Apart from shepherding Mission: Quality, I was the chairman of the sales and marketing council of the corporation and the chairman of the information systems council. Additionally, I was on the board of Wipro GE Medical Systems, the joint venture I had briefly worked at. I was also a member of the corporate executive council that was the apex body overseeing strategy and the roll-out of key initiatives across the various divisions. What more could a man like me ask for? Yet, there was a deep void growing inside, making me vulnerable without my even knowing it. Perhaps, it was the onset of a mid-life transition that is designed to make you conclude that your life is half-empty, not half-full. Perhaps, there were some systemic reasons within the organization and some personal issues.

Looking back, I realize I had several peeves. First and foremost, I was unhappy with the leadership of the different businesses and their individual styles and varying adoption of change. The Six Sigma movement was fraught with issues, not as a basic quality standard but in becoming a way of life. One of the reasons behind this lack of alignment was Premji's inability to answer clearly what was in it for people to achieve the goal of making Wipro world-class. Remember, at that time, Wipro did not practise shared wealth creation in any significant way. It did not do so until 1999.

In addition to all that, Premji believed in loading everyone with disparate responsibilities, and had a tendency to micro-manage. Part of my job was to sit with him in business unit reviews where hours were spent grilling business unit managers, discussing mundane operational issues. I did not enjoy this.

Finally, I was also unhappy with the way my promotions had been handled. First, I was given the designation vice president international technology division, then I became chief executive of global R&D and then I became corporate vice president—these were three consecutive assignments and in each I had obviously done very well. To the outside world I was prospering, yet, viewed from a competency band, the three designations meant no change in level. I sensed a lack of grace on the part of a system I had helped build.

But the question that comes up is: Does all this really

justify leaving an organization at the prime of one's career? Maybe, maybe not. With hindsight I believe that because of the vulnerability of my age, each of these peeves got magnified in importance. After all, once you decide to be unhappy, even a small irritation becomes a great annoyance.

In September that year Lucent Technologies got in touch with me and offered me a position, selling it to me as a role 'like that of a chief operating officer', to help set up Bell Labs in India. In November, I told Premji to look for a substitute. After five months of back and forth, on 1 April 1998 I left Wipro. It was my life's singular attempt at irrevocable, professional self-destruction.

PART III

CHAPTER 18

The Pain of Rebirth

With hindsight my decision to join Lucent Technologies was a bad one and the blame is largely mine. It is interesting how high achievers bent upon making a wrong decision produce convincing arguments and these then begin to take on a life of their own. I had spent ten years in Wipro and in that time had learnt many things. One of the high points during those years was the time I spent in the corporate office during which I learnt about Total Quality Management. Now I wanted to learn all about Innovation, because it was the next frontier. What better place, I argued, than Bell Labs which filed nearly 3.5 patents a day? Bell Labs, after the split from AT&T, was now owned by Lucent and one division was setting up a software development centre in

Bangalore. The people who 'sold' me the job did suggest that it was the Bell Lab Development Center. In reality, it had nothing to do with the legendary Bell Labs and all the assignment required was a middle-level manager to assist the head of the centre, an expatriate manager from the US. It took me exactly a week to realize that it was yet another multinational company's software development centre with the additional twist of being an extremely political organization. Each day at work became increasingly difficult for me. But hadn't I been responsible for choosing this company, the change in my career and an environment that wasn't right for me? Why had I not done due diligence before taking the bait?

In the Panchatantra, there is a story of a poor Brahmin who sees an old tiger in a forest. The tiger has a golden bangle in his paws and offers it to the man. The man is frightened and doesn't want to go near the tiger. The tiger moans that he is too old to hunt and kill and is now at the end of his life. He is toothless and his claws have all but fallen. The tiger wants to make penance by offering the bangle to a good man so that he can atone for a life of violence. He requests the Brahmin to take a dip in the pond nearby and receive the bangle from him so that he can breathe his last. The animal sounds so genuine, the poor Brahmin pities the tiger; he believes the story. He enters the pond, only to get stuck in the mud. The tiger promptly devours the Brahmin. The question is: Who killed the man? Is it the tiger or the man's greed?

What were the real factors that pushed me to change

my job? I can add more reasons to the list, apart from the ones given earlier. In reality, high achievers are also their worst enemies and sometimes make near-fatal mistakes. I was going through a mid-life transition whose impact neither I nor the organization I worked for understood. Some of the issues that bothered me could have been raised by me candidly; some would have sorted themselves out in time. The solution did not lie in accepting an assignment in an organization I was temperamentally not suited for. It was too large a risk at forty.

As the ghost of Innovation started to take on a life of its own within me, I went a step further. I told people that I would work for just five more years, focussing on Innovation as a theme, and then move on to doing four things for the rest of my life: read, write, travel and teach. I was romanticizing the idea. But look at the inherent stupidity of the idea: given today's life expectancy, people work well past their sixties! And here I was, saying that I would hang up my boots at forty-five. On top of that, do reading, writing, travelling and teaching really require a job change? Doesn't any senior-level corporate job allow you enough time to do these things without the need to quit altogether? But who can argue with one's own self?

I sold three hundred vested Wipro shares for three hundred rupees each and walked out of another two thousand shares that were unvested. In the following three years, the value of that holding, after several splits, would have been worth a few million dollars, thanks to how Wipro's stock fared. When I joined Lucent, its shares were trading at around hundred dollars a piece. In the same period, their price went down to one dollar a share. While my salary at Wipro was half of what Lucent paid me, the stock gain would have covered the salary differential a few hundred times over. But all this is realization with hindsight. At that moment, when I changed jobs, I wanted to learn about Innovation.

¤

Saying goodbye to senior colleagues at Wipro was not difficult. It was devastating saying goodbye to the thousands of junior colleagues who looked up to me. Many thought of me as a role model. In a telling moment, one colleague, Tanaz Kadwa, barged into my room. She was in anger and pain and about to cry. She looked me sternly in the eye and said, 'So, even god has feet of clay,' and without waiting for my response, left, banging the door behind her. I was speechless; I was guilty and judgement had been delivered.

There is nothing more painful in life than to see your gods fail. The teacher you once loved and respected and considered the last post of integrity turns out to be an ordinary, vulnerable, favour-seeking man. The honest-to-the-core role model in the family turns out to be nothing more than a self-serving individual putting on a façade, whose sense of morality is specific to a given time and space. It is the inevitability of growing up without which we cannot become complete human beings.

Yet, I feel the convulsion each time my gods fail. And many years after Tanaz stormed out of my room, I remember how I failed Tanaz.

¤

Azim Premji had warned me that I would have a tough time dealing with internal politics in a large multinational company and he turned out to be prophetically accurate. On the one hand, India was opening up to many great opportunities and, on the other, internal power play among Lucent's many business units made it difficult for the company to scale new heights in India. It was clear to me that I was wasting my time. Though joining Lucent turned out to be a poor decision, the time I spent there was useful in two ways: it gave me the opportunity to reflect on the emerging service economy and the role Indian software companies would play in it. It also caused enough pain for me to pursue the idea of starting out on my own. Nothing works better than the promise of a great future and the simultaneous sensation of standing on a burning bridge.

On 17 June 1998 I reached out to Krishna Kumar (KK), an erstwhile colleague at Wipro, who was chief executive of their newly formed electronic commerce division. I had great admiration for KK. I had watched him work from a distance and felt that the two of us would make a great team. Following a phone conversation, we met in Karavali restaurant in Bangalore for lunch. There we agreed that we were destined for something larger than what we were both doing and decided to create an aspirational organization that would be higher up the value chain; an organization that would be value-centric, socially connected and based on the principle of shared wealth creation. The idea of MindTree germinated that day. As MindTree was born and grew over the course of the next decade, it seems to us that it is indeed the purpose for which life was preparing us, one experience at a time. For me, MindTree became the bridge between who I was and who I was meant to be, from making it big in life to making it good.

CHAPTER 19

The Joy of Being Reborn

At first, it was just a dream. Between June and August of 1998, KK and I met almost every night. On weekends, he and I would take our bikes and go cycling into the wilderness behind the development where we lived. We would sit under huge raintrees, talking about how to set up a great company. We decided to expand the group of co-founders and I spoke to Namakkal Parthasarathy whom I had left behind at Wipro's global R&D division. We also reached out to a couple of venture capitalists who showed preliminary interest in our ideas. In August that year, my work took me to New Jersey where Lucent had its headquarters. A chance meeting there with Anjan Lahiri, an ex-colleague who had migrated to the US, led to the expansion of the seed team. Through Anjan, we added Kamran Ozair and Scott Staples to the team. They were working with Anjan at Cambridge Technology Partners. On my return to India, I spoke to my colleague Rostow Ravanan at Lucent and he readily agreed to join as the finance expert. An ex-KPMG hand, he brought strategy and finance knowledge that the team would need in the days to come.

We decided to get together as a team to flesh out the mission, vision and values of the company of our dreams. We took time off from our respective jobs and drove down to Visakhapatnam on the Bay of Bengal coast, a little more than a thousand kilometres by road from Bangalore. For over a decade, I had been fascinated with the beach there—my first visit was on behalf of PSI to present a plan to the Indian Railways for computerizing locomotive maintenance. I had fallen in love with the beauty and seclusion of the rocks along the coastline. There was something special about the place; for some reason, I liked to think of it as a sacred space. Come Christmas Eve 1998, we drove down in two cars all the way from Bangalore; Anjan flew down from the US. We holed up at The Park hotel for a whole week—it was where I had stayed on my first visit. We took breaks only to eat and sleep; the conversations were intense. We plastered conference room walls with ideas on flip-charts. We took turns at facilitating discussions on how to match our individual needs, our personal goals, our strengths and limitations. We talked about the unfolding opportunities around us and what it would take to create value out of them and then spoke about the mission, vision, values and differentiation for the yet-to-be-born corporation. At the end, we thrashed out a preliminary business plan. Armed with a PowerPoint presentation, we returned, to start scouting for venture capital.

By February 1999, the list of venture capitalists we were talking to had grown. It was some coincidence that two old friends, Som Das and Sudhir Sethi, had in the meantime joined Walden International, a Silicon Valley venture firm. Som and Sudhir started showing interest and encouraged us to fine-tune the business plan. In March, I was again sent to the US and met Som and Sudhir to close the deal but what Som told me sent me for a spin—Ashok Soota had decided to leave Wipro to begin something on his own. Ashok and Som's acquaintance went back to the latter's days at VLSI and Ashok had asked if Walden would be interested in funding him. Som had agreed in principle but had also told Ashok that someone he knew well had progressed significantly on a similar plan with Walden. Ashok being Ashok, had guessed that it was me. Som suggested Ashok combine forces with us to build one company. Ashok thought that Som should speak with me first. It was a miracle. No one in his senses would ever have imagined Ashok leaving Wipro! Here was one of the most respected people in the industry willing to join hands with us! It took no time for KK, Rostow, Partha, Anjan and I to confabulate on this new possibility. Scott and Kamran did not know Ashok and had very little understanding of the dynamic, leaving their part of the thinking to Anjan. We all agreed that Ashok would be the perfect leader for us and we intimated Walden that we would merge our ambitions and, all things being equal, would like them to be the lead venture capitalist. We got our second venture partner, V.G. Siddhartha of Global Technology Partners, with Ashok's coming on board. (Siddhartha went on to found the Café Coffee Day chain.) We settled the valuation of the company and raised 9.5 million dollars by giving away 44 per cent of the company. We kept aside 16.67 per cent of the ownership for future employees; the rest was to be held by the founders.

When word broke in July that Ashok was quitting Wipro and that we were coming together to form a new company, the story hit the headlines. For weeks together Bangalore was agog with excitement. Prior to Ashok coming on board, I had reached out to Kalyan Banerjee, another ex-colleague at Wipro, who had promptly agreed to join. After Ashok's decision to leave Wipro, Srinivasan Janakiraman, known as Jani, who was at the time chief executive of Wipro's global R&D, was desolate. When I had moved out of there to join Premji's office, I had handed over the mantle of chief executive of global R&D to Jani. He told Ashok that with my departure from Wipro, he had lost one wing and now with Ashok going away, the other one had been clipped. He just didn't want to stay behind at Wipro. Ashok asked me to meet him to talk him out of the idea or get him in as the tenth co-founder. Consequently, Jani and I met at Cubbon Park in Bangalore and after a short conversation it was clear that our paths were destined to be the same. With Jani, the founding team was complete.

Years later, it has become clear to me that professional respect for each other, a shared value system and middle-class upbringing is the glue that has held this team together. We all come from very modest backgrounds. And all of us are first-generation entrepreneurs.

Ashok's father was a colonel in the Indian Army. KK's father was a doctor in the railways. Jani's father was a village postmaster. Partha's father was a travelling ticket collector on trains. Rostow's father was an accountant in a brewery. Kalyan's father became a geologist and spent all his life in the coal mines. Scott's father was an air force pilot who eventually changed careers to become an accountant and his mother was an elementary school teacher. Anjan's father served in the army and Kamran's father was a civil engineer in Pakistan. Looking back, our past gave us an unspoken code of conduct, a certain inbuilt capacity to work hard and a shared understanding of why we had decided to be in this together.

After Ashok came on board, we revisited the business plan several times: it was now time to find a name for the company. We decided to go about it in a professional manner, engaging a company in California called Name It that went through our mission, vision, values and business plan and then engaged their contributors all over the world—they came up with 729 possible names. From these, we whittled down a shortlist of ten and voted for MindTree. Later, a friend of Ashok told us to our delight that MindTree is *manovriksha* in the Upanishads—the eternal provider of intellectual solutions! With the name chosen, we now had to think of a visual identity. We decided to ask a group of children with cerebral palsy at the Spastic Society of Karnataka to come up with the visual.

¤

My personal association with the cause of cerebral palsy started when I returned from the US in 1993. While working in the Valley, I was amazed to see the extent of corporate involvement in local communities. Many corporations took active interest in local affairs, in issues ranging from education to health to affirmative action. The idea went well beyond charity; it was about creating inclusion, learning from each other and harnessing the power of the organization to channel volunteerism. On my return I requested Dr Mitta to give me a cause to work on, in addition to my job at Wipro. He introduced me to the Spastic Society of Karnataka. I had no idea about cerebral palsy, autism or other such neuro-muscular conditions.

During my very first visit to the Spastic Society school in Bangalore, I met Sheena Watson, a visiting art teacher from Ireland. She was painstakingly trying to teach young children with cerebral palsy to hold a paintbrush. For her, it was not just an effort to make the children creative; it was therapy for a more fundamental problem—muscular control. For each of these children, holding the brush was an effort to teach the hand, eyes and face to obey the brain. I stood transfixed as each child held the brush, dipped it in paint and laboured to produce brilliant pieces of art. Probably because many of these children cannot speak or express themselves without severe effort, their paintings have extraordinary vibrancy. The colours are spectacular and spontaneous—as if compensating for the gaps of an unseen god. It was also a moment of great self-realization for me. These children were, as they were painting, not focussed on their disability but on their dreams.

While thinking through the formation of the company, we had not only thought through our mission, vision and values, we had also decided that our DNA would be imagination, action and joy. Weeks before the launch of MindTree, when we had decided to speak to the Spastic Society of Karnataka, we asked them to allow us to interact with the children for a week so that we could explain to them the idea of MindTree and then work with them to create the visual identity of the company based on the DNA of imagination, action and joy.

After a few days of running a workshop on what is a company, why a company has a logo and, above all, what kind of company MindTree intended to become, the children got down to designing. Initial designs were disappointing. The children had understood the word MindTree quite literally. But we did not give up. Another workshop was conducted to give the children an appreciation of many famous logos and they were encouraged to discover subliminal meaning in them: they were required to interpret values in the visual identity of a brand. Then the magic happened. Something clicked, as if a combination lock had suddenly snapped open in their minds. From labour on their faces, we could now see the delight of discovery. From among the ten designs we received, it wasn't difficult to pick up the astounding work of seventeen-year-old Chetan, who said in support of his work that the upward blue stroke in his creation stood for limitless imagination, the red background denoted action and the yellows were 'bubbles of joy'.

As a token of our appreciation, we gifted five thousand shares of MindTree to the Spastic Society of Karnataka. Another student, Latha, who had captivated us with her smile, became our first receptionist. When Bill Clinton visited India as President of the United States of America and met with CEOs of IT companies, we took Chetan along to meet him. President Clinton autographed Chetan's logo. Every MindTree facility we have subsequently designed is a museum of art produced by the children of the Spastic Society of Karnataka.

¤

Having tied up the founding team, the venture capital, the name and the logo, MindTree opened for business on 18 August 1999. Ashok Soota was chairman, I was chief operating officer, KK took on the role of president of IT services and Jani as president of the R&D services business. Everyone got down to work pretty quickly. Partha took on the task of delivery for KK's business and

Kalyan worked on setting up the training, development and knowledge management functions. Scott, Anjan and Kamran got busy setting up the US operations. The IT services business had decided to focus on Internet-related technologies and the R&D business had opted to focus on the telecom industry as these were the blazing sectors of the day. We felt that these two areas would give us a unique position along with our capability to provide IT strategy consulting, something Indian players were not in a position to deliver. But the critical task at hand was to set up a team so that the organization could expand rapidly. Thanks to personal relationships and reputations built over time, each of us could attract outstanding individuals in various fields. Ashok had said that the first five hundred MindTree Minds should all be seen as co-founders—so everyone who came on board was treated with the same respect and offered significant challenge to be his or her best. In order to get them involved in the institution-building effort, we decided to revisit the values that had been crafted at Visakhapatnam. Ashok and I travelled to every location, met each individual and asked them to define the kind of company they wanted to create. This led to the creation of the MindTree values: Caring, Learning, Achieving, Sharing and Social Responsibility (CLASS). These values went on to not only bind us as a people, they proved to be immensely valuable in times of great difficulty.

The founding team's diversity and at the same time a sense of shared heritage helped attract a certain kind of leadership at the next level. Erik Mann,

R.K. Veeraraghavan, Joe King, Raja Shanmugam, Raj Datta, Amit Agrawal, Abraham Moses and Babuji Philip Abraham are all persons who made the idea of MindTree fractal and expanded the circle of believers. Each is a very unique individual who has shaped MindTree and held on to the core in times of great adversity. These are people who did not ask for assurances, they became the assurance.

Erik Mann's mother had escaped Communist East Germany in 1953 and come to the US where she met his father who ran a family furniture repair business in Brooklyn. Growing up in Brooklyn, Erik went to Princeton, partly paying for his own education, working as a waiter and giving tennis lessons over the weekend. He had enrolled to study aeronautical engineering (even today he is a serious cross-country glider pilot), but when Princeton decided to move away from hands-on flight research, he shifted to the study of the history of science. After joining the IT industry, Erik eventually moved to Cambridge Technology Partners from where he came to MindTree. Erik rose to become the founder of MindTree's insurance industry group that contributed 12 per cent of MindTree's revenues in 2008.

R.K. Veeraraghavan was born in a lower-middle-class family in Chennai and grew up with a polio-affected leg. His biggest ambition in life was to ride a bicycle. The day he could do that, he knew he could do anything. Veera, as we call him, graduated from BITS, Pilani and worked for Wipro before he came on board and today he is the global delivery head at MindTree.

Joe King was born and raised in the Bronx in New York until he was five. His father was a teacher for twenty-three years. Joe recalls how sometimes he was the only white in a black neighbourhood! Joe paid for his college education. Starting professional life by selling computer stationery in New York City, he completed his MBA at Fordham and today he leads MindTree's global marketing function.

Raja Shanmugam assembled the furniture with his own hands when MindTree's California office started. Raja's mother had gone to a government hospital in Salem, Tamil Nadu at the time of his birth. The hospital refused to admit her since she had arrived before the hospital opened for the day. They turned her away. Raja would not wait: his mother delivered him by the roadside. Raja's unusual arrival into the world earned him the nickname Mannalandan from his grandmother—literally 'One who measures the Earth'. Today, he's head of the Asia-Pacific region.

Raj Datta was born in India and raised in Africa and then in the US, with a small stint with an Indian guru at an ashram near Mumbai. He found his calling when he went to study at Cornell and developed his fascination for open source software. His life's goal was to work in the area of knowledge management and he leads our effort in that area, making MindTree one of the youngest entrants into the Most Admired Knowledge Enterprise (MAKE) club.

Unlike Raj who left India as a child, Amit Agrawal was born in the US of immigrant Indian parents and growing up had very little idea about India. Admittedly, MindTree became his first real exposure to India. At college in Rutgers, Amit enrolled for a double major in engineering and music, seriously toying for a while with the idea of composing music before deciding on computer science and ended up at Cambridge Technology Partners. There he met Anjan, Scott and Kamran. Amit helped deliver our first few projects as a technical architect, moved from the east to the west coast and eventually went to Florida to lead our relationship with Burger King.

Abraham Moses was one of eight children when his father retired as a junior commissioned officer in the army; there was little food for the family at home. He is proud to say, every time, that he started life as a coolie. From there, he built his life one step at a time and worked with me at Wipro's global R&D division managing administrative functions. There was something special about the man's soul because he led all our engagements with orphanages and homes for the dying and the destitute, was always the first to help whenever anyone needed some, and yet would be the first to arrive and the last to leave the workplace. When I left Wipro I had told him our parting was going to be temporary.

The one leader whose arrival at MindTree will always remain unique is that of Babuji Philip Abraham. Early in the life of MindTree, one day, Prasad, at the time the head of people function, came running into my office. He led me towards the conference room where a group of eight people were seated. 'They want to join MindTree,'

he said. 'But before they do, they want to interview *you*.'
MindTree had just been launched. A group of engineers
working under Babuji for years at Verifone (later HP)
had caught the start-up bug and heard the MindTree
story. 'We are going to check them out. Do you want to
come?' they asked Babuji. The eight showed up en masse
at our makeshift office, checked us out and then chorused
that they were ready to be given their job offers! We
could not make a collective offer; we had to split them
up—after all, compensation and benefits must be personal
to every individual. Babuji remains one of the most
popular leaders among MindTree Minds.

¤

Our first full financial year was a home run. We overshot
our plans and closed the year at 9.5 million dollars. The
second year got off to a good start. Business poured in,
though the R&D business was taking more time to set
itself up because the large telecom players were all
locked in multi-year deals with existing service providers.
The tried-and-tested route of securing project business
was not working out. Unfazed, we started setting up our
own intellectual property programme led by Sharmila
Saha. She put the plan together, a group of young
engineers was assembled under her tutelage and we
started working in the area of short-range wireless. That
effort was to blossom in subsequent years making
MindTree one of the top three providers in the world of
Bluetooth protocol stack technology with licensees like

Sony and NEC in Japan, Logitech in the US, GN Net in Denmark and many others.

Amidst all this, two things started to happen: one, we began the process of raising our second round of funding because we knew it would be a long-drawn affair. Like the first round it would involve several rounds of discussion, negotiation and mutual due diligence. This time though we expected it to be more intense because there was a business already on the ground, thereby lending itself to higher scrutiny, quite unlike the first time when all we could have been asked was questions on a business plan. As the match-making process started and a few suitors arrived, the early signs of the dot-com bust, telecom slowdown and a possible US recession appeared on the horizon.

This was also the time we sensed signs of misalignment within our own organization.

CHAPTER 20

Leadership in a Time of Crisis

Though MindTree got off to a great start under Ashok's overall leadership, in reality the extended team was not perfectly aligned from day one. With people from many different national origins, there were hiccups in understanding each other due to both professional and cultural diversities. There were also integration issues caused by the fact that we were trying to build a company that would combine IT strategy consulting with traditional software development. The former is very individualistic, methodology dependent and style led while the latter builds on teamwork, process maturity and is substance led. The problem of alignment began to surface as MindTree became successful very rapidly. As small signs of lack of integration began to surface, it was decided that I would move to the US and in the spring of 2001 I returned to the US. In many ways, my arrival in the US could not have been better and worse timed.

On my first day at MindTree's Somerville office, as I was going up in the elevator, a group of Americans were looking at me with keen interest and then one of them asked, 'Are you not the one relocating to New Jersey?' That same day, the *New York Times* had carried a half-page article on MindTree, with a photograph of Ashok and me. The article was captioned 'A Different Kind of Company'—just what we wanted to be known as—and it went on to say that Subroto Bagchi was relocating to the US as part of the overall strategy. Pleased as I was with the prop, I had no idea that I would soon have to preside over not the alignment of the core, but the preservation of faith itself.

Once I came on board, the primary task on hand was to move the office to a cheaper location. We had signed an ugly lease for a proposed new office that had a quarter of a million dollars stuck as security deposit and the builder was taking us for a ride with expenses that would mean another similar amount for fit-outs. The business simply was not going to be able to afford it. This was no time to splurge. We decided that we would rescind the deal and knowing that we may lose the deposited money (which we eventually did) we needed to move the office to a significantly cheaper location against popular will. After some scouting around, we settled on a rather boxy but more affordable place in Somerset, New Jersey. It was a bare, forty thousand square feet floor in a multi-tenant office building. New fit-outs and furniture could potentially cost close to seven hundred and fifty thousand dollars! The next weekend, I went to New York City and bought out second-hand furniture from a financial services company that was shutting down. For less than fifty thousand dollars, we bought all the partitions, tables and chairs and were ready to go.

The next thing on my agenda was to get the leadership team to get to know each other better and build a shared vision of the future. It was a high performance team in which everyone was individually great but, collectively, the team members were beginning to show signs of strain. I also needed to open up communication at a business level; I needed them to think like owners of a business and not as high performers in silos. The team needed to build empathy for what the other person was doing. Erik knew a friend who rented shore houses on the beach during the summer. We went there and locked in for a couple of days. The team cooked all the meals together, slept on the floor and on the sofa, worked out issues, talked about what they liked and disliked about each other, discussed key business priorities and a vision for the collective future as they drank wine and smoked cigars in the evening after dinner and the dishes were done.

Many years later, I read Otto Scharmer's book *Theory U* that reminded me of the sessions at the shore house. In many ways, our work during the two days was like travelling 'through the U' as Scharmer tells you—an experience of 'sensing' in the beginning as you travel down the U, 'presencing' as you settle at the bottom and then the experience of 'realizing' as you move up the right side of the U. The process is what he calls 'leading from the future'. As you move from sensing to presencing, you first learn to let go, before you can 'let come'. Answers often jump out of the stillness of your mind. MindTree leaders went through that experience and now they were ready for action. Well, almost.

This time spent together was very beneficial for the team as a whole, although there was one member who just didn't seem to fit in. I had to finally fire this member who was neither producing results nor making the effort to be a core part of the leadership team. The parting was not pleasant, but in the long run it was the best course of action I could have taken. Sometimes, our gut instinct tells us that the job and the person are a wrong fit; however much we try to work it out, there's always something missing. More often than not, such persons behave or act in a manner which makes the decision to ask them to leave easier.

The next few months saw a lot of activity on all fronts. I introduced a monthly operations review for the leaders. Everyone now got the same view of business that I had. I met with every single MindTree Mind, together with my finance and human resource people. I looked at every aspect of compliance for the office operations. I went out and met with my customers and listened to them. Back in India, we were busy trying to raise a second round of funding. In reality, the decision had almost been taken: we knew whom we were going to raise the money from and on what terms, but the money had not come into the bank account. Between August 1999 and July 2000, we had managed well with the 9.5 million dollars we had raised from our first round of venture capital funding. This time, the actual fund raising had taken almost six months of serious conversation with potential investors. We had not run out of money yet but at the same time we needed to raise some soon enough to last us for the next couple of years. Ashok was clear that we would not take the company public in a hurry. Thus, it was important to close the second round of funding. It finally reached us, providentially, in August 2001. We had a board meeting around that time, and as an upbeat team we revised our five-year targets upwards. Little did we know that a month from then the whole world would come to a standstill!

¤

On 11 September 2001, I was on a visit to our Bangalore office. Late in the afternoon, Babuji Abraham, usually the alert system of the corporation, sent me a message saying a plane had crashed into the World Trade Center. Nothing more was forthcoming. I was unsure what to make of the news. After a while, I left for dinner with the first MBA batch to join MindTree. These were graduates of the class of 2000. I knew them well and they wanted to try their newly acquired culinary skills on me. I went to the apartment in which they were planning the community dinner. The television was on. The moment I entered, I saw the second plane hit the twin towers.

The dinner was called off. I returned to office and video conferenced with Scott Staples, who was officiating in my absence. Two MindTree Minds were missing. It was completely chaotic because cell phones were not working in New York City. Hours later, they were traced; one had run down the staircase and the other had taken the elevator even as the second plane was about to crash into the second tower. Though the two were safe, we unfortunately lost our customer with whom they were working at the time.

The next day, I flew back to the US. My connecting flight to Newark had four passengers including myself. The world had indeed changed forever. For weeks to follow, the conversation was about the debris, body parts, fire engines and funerals, of hopelessness and of clinging on to hope. Everyone knew someone who had lost a loved one. Corporate America, still in the throes of the dot-com and telecom bust and the economic slowdown, was in a complete state of shock. Fear and uncertainty were writ large everywhere. In the MindTree office, I could sense an invisible pall of toxic gloom and that needed to be lifted. Business was not the most important item of the agenda on hand. We needed to detoxify the leadership team. For that, I needed help.

¤

Raghu Garud taught strategy at the Stern School, New York University. When we started MindTree, he had approached Ashok with an interesting idea. Having co-authored a book titled *The Innovation Engine* after years of looking at 3M as a company, he was now interested in studying a start-up which could be a potential success-in-the-making. According to him, too many companies were researched after becoming great. He and his colleagues wanted to look under the hood of something that was a work-in-progress. We had readily agreed to the idea. Their project was called the 'Mindful Mirror'. As part of this exercise, Raghu and Professor Roger Dunbar periodically interacted with us in order to understand what we were doing.

I went to Raghu and Roger and asked them for help. They understood my predicament. Both men had deep empathy for MindTree. Though they had, as academics, adopted us to track our progress, now I was asking them to be players. We crossed a line that day. We wanted to seek answers to various questions which we thought the leaders would be grappling with: What was going to unfold? How would it affect them? How does such trauma affect us? What was right and wrong at a time like this? We felt if we could aid the leaders to make sense of a time like this, the next step would be to get them to take charge of others. Raghu and Roger suggested that we needed to do three things: ask the leaders to spell out what was on their mind; take them through a famous management case study on leadership in times of disaster; and, finally, I would have to show the way forward.

I asked every leader to list out the issues that were on his or her mind. On 20 October 2001, we sat around a table, facilitated by Raghu and Roger. Like a dam bursting, the issues poured out from the leaders:

'The uncertainty surrounding continued employment is extremely stressful as I represent the single source of income for my family.'

'I feel tremendous uncertainty about meeting our revenue and profitability targets. The numbers were ambitious one year ago, but with the nosedive our industry has taken since the recent terrorist attacks, the stated goals appear impossible to achieve.'

'How long can the company survive as it is presently organized?'

'What will the future organization look like and what role, if any, will I have in the organization?'

'I am not intimately familiar with our financials but I am concerned that we are losing money across most geographies. This leads to the somewhat frightful prospect that we might not be around for long!!!'

The questions kept flowing: How would the actions in Afghanistan affect our business? Would India be perceived by ignorant US buyers as 'Middle Eastern'? Would they hold a bias against doing business with that part of the world? Had we set up our company to focus on the wrong things? How far would pricing go down and what final effect would this have on salaries? There was no question that we were working hard, but were we working smart? Was this a temporary phase or was this an adjustment of the industry to where it really belonged? With so many companies going out of business and new business hard to come by, did we have the staying power to ride out the storm? How long would we be able to continue before we ran out of money?

After hours of discussion, it was clear that no one really had the definitive answer and as a result no one truly understood his or her consequent role. At this stage, we took a break and Raghu and Roger handed out the famous Uruguayan team's air-crash case study. In October 1972, an Uruguayan rugby team had chartered a Fairchild F-227 to get to Chile. Flying over Argentina, the plane met with rough weather over the Andes and crashed and many aboard died on a snowbound peak. The people who were in the fuselage escaped miraculously as the rear section slid out on the snow. What followed is a tale of hope and hopelessness as the survivors went through a seventy-two-day ordeal during which they had to, at one stage, eat the flesh of their dead compatriots in order to stay alive. Through this real story of courage and determination, a powerful leadership lesson emerged. Through the course of the crash and the return to civilization, those who finally made it underwent live lessons in leadership, emergent in a situational manner, witnessing power shifts within the group from one phase to the next.

An intense conversation took place around the case study and we linked it constantly to the issues the leaders had raised about MindTree's current and future state. It was clear to everyone that we were all dealing with something quite akin to an unscripted mountain crash.

Right at this moment, the uncertainty we faced was close to the reality of survival at thirteen thousand feet in icy conditions. It also drove home the point that no single leader could bring us back to civilization. That, like the seventy-two-day-ordeal, would have to be dealt with one day at a time. We also started to realize that in different parts of the dramatic journey ahead, different people would have to bring to bear their situational leadership capabilities.

At the end, I made an hour-long presentation titled 'Leading Continuity' on the way forward. It summarized my understanding of the challenges of the hour and what I expected my leaders to bring to the table. I believed that the actions of the US government would have wider, larger implications for everyone. The role of governments stood re-legitimized everywhere in the wake of 9/11. This would bring back a sense of forced normalcy and I saw that as a near-term inevitability. I also felt that the recession would ease in the latter half of 2002 and pent-up demand would have to bring back growth. New areas like biotech, biometrics and bio-defence would gain momentum. I told my team that the Internet would return. It had to. I believed that the IPO markets would reappear after 2003 and there would be fresh momentum for outsourcing. Blue-sky projects had to give way to operation-intensive and mission-critical applications. I also felt that competition and price pressure would go up and profitability would come down. While giving up inefficiencies, new efficiencies needed to be introduced. Business models had to change, wage normalization was inevitable—after all, wages had gone up artificially during the go-go days and needed to return to earth. In the near term, I saw venture capital drying up. I also saw the need for reskilling at all levels at a time like this. It was clear that while people would hire again, less people would be needed to do more things.

Given the overall position, I felt our leaders needed to focus on sustaining the cash through the long winter, and streamlining our billing and collection to make sure that operational cash flow was not affected. We needed to focus on profitability, cut the flab wherever possible. We needed to push more business overseas, go after larger deals, dig deeper with the existing large accounts and to leverage like hell. I asked that we acquire new customers in new areas and choose our customers well, reskill ourselves, keep the perspective and have fun.

Faced with a crisis, the job of a leader is to take charge and broadcast his or her intent. It is not a time for self-pity, not a time to ask, 'Why me?' In the middle of adversity, a leader must see what can be saved and what must be given up. Everything during such a period is negotiable. In times of such great upheaval, a leader must learn to compartmentalize issues. A leader can share some of his pain with those he loves but he cannot overburden anyone with what only he must bear. Apparent solutions do not work in such times and no known solution may exist.

One has to be brave enough to try and, sometimes, fail.

Mother Teresa once said, 'God does not require us to succeed, he only asks us to try.'

Finally, in the worst of times, the job of a leader is to let his or her people know that there is a tomorrow.

¤

Time moved slowly. In February of 2002, I got a call from India that mother had suffered a serious stroke. I had left her with Dadamoni who was now the chief secretary of Orissa. She had been admitted to the Capital Hospital there. It was the main government hospital. Though not the best equipped, it still had good doctors. When someone suggested that she be taken to a state-of-the-art private hospital in town, Dadamoni refused. 'If the chief secretary to the government does not have faith in his own health care system, what message will that send to the people who have no choice but to depend on it?' he asked.

I flew down to Bhubaneswar to see her. She was clearly struggling. Her fair skin had crumpled, one side of her face was in a state of paralysis, her speech was affected and when she spoke she was incoherent. She was at the end of her journey, but not there yet. I stayed by her side for two weeks. My mornings began at the hospital. I would stay until night, going home during the day only for lunch. Every day, the nurses came, sponged her, fed her, gave her her medicines. Then the doctors came as per their routine and they all said the same thing—she is at an advanced age, has suffered a massive stroke, no one can really say what will happen, the brain often has miraculous ways in which it recovers from something like this, a doctor's job is to support through medication and not play god. After a few days, we learnt not to blabber our anxiety.

Two weeks passed. Finally, I decided to go back to the United States. She herself would have disapproved of my abandoning work to hover around her without the capability to help in anyway. On my last day in Bhubaneswar, I went to a temple and prayed that she be given safe passage. On my way to the airport, I stopped to kiss her goodbye one last time. That is when she simply told me, 'Go, kiss the world.'

In the days and weeks that followed, she deteriorated but she endured it all with no complaints. Finally, come summer, she moved on. Unlike the time when father had died, I was not at hand. But it did not matter because she had emptied herself completely in me, filling me to the brim and flowing over. Now, she, I and the whole world had become one.

CHAPTER 21

Tomorrow Always Comes

Moving on from the aftermath of 9/11, when tomorrow did come, it brought more bad news than good news. In retaliation of the attack on the Twin Towers, the United States began bombing Afghanistan. After a few months, there was an outbreak of the SARS epidemic in Asia that brought business travel to a standstill. The US economic slowdown became a full-blown recession and extended itself to the rest of the world. George Bush invaded Iraq to dig out weapons of mass destruction that did not exist. Choosing this as the most appropriate time for hostility, India and Pakistan decided to go to war with nuclear swagger. This could have been the predictable, perfect stage for MindTree to shut down like many hundreds of companies born in the same time and space.

What saved us were Ashok Soota's unwavering leadership that did not have the word 'panic' in the lexicon, the alignment of the core team around the values MindTree stood for, the confidence our top three customers—Avis, Franklin Templeton and Unilever—had in us, companies that did not cutback on spending and, finally, the fact that the fourteen million dollars we had raised during our second-round funding was intact in the bank. Telling ourselves that MindTree was all we had, we went about our business without despair. Even then it seemed as if the future was a brick wall. But then, someone has said, it is meant to be that way: a brick wall is there to keep out people who really do not want to go beyond it.

Our business depended heavily on new software development. Faced with uncertain times, companies scaled back all new development. Their budgets shifted to software maintenance that could result in cost reduction. At the same time, chief information officers of leading companies sought to protect themselves by aligning with 'safer' choices, going to large Indian or American firms and staying away from fledgling companies. In this overall gloom and doom, I distinctly remember two interesting events. One was a briefing session I had with an analyst of a global research firm. After a spirited presentation by me, he had only one redeeming comment to make: by 2005, only those software services companies that had sales greater than a billion dollars would survive! I thanked him for writing our epitaph. The man lost his job in the following cutback.

The other interesting event took place when Avis, our number one customer, went through a series of top-level changes. A hurricane of a new CEO came to 'fix' the place and played havoc with the IT organization. We got badly entangled with the sputtering launch of Avis.com—their most significant online revenue engine. A new chief information officer was appointed and he asked to see him. He had heard a few negative things linking us to the problematic launch of Avis's new reservation site. When he greeted me, he said, 'From what I hear about you, I should actually be showing you the door.' I instantly liked the man for his candour. Raj Rawal was an ex-GE executive who ran his own consulting organization that rented chief information officers to turnaround IT organizations in difficulty. After these officers put the corporations back on track, they helped find full-time chief information officers and then moved on. As I settled down in a chair, I told Raj that I also wanted to have a definitive conversation about the relationship. 'Raj, I would rather die once than die every day.' Raj liked my stance. He placed his trust in us. Things moved north, their business boomed and we survived. In time, Raj moved on and became the chief information officer at Burger King. We went on to build great applications there. Thanks to the work we were doing at Avis, we developed many large and complex applications for organizations such as Cendant, Avis's holding company, the International Air Transport Association (IATA) and Travel Click. But it was our deal with Volvo in 2002 that changed everything. Volvo had chosen us because they wanted to work with a mid-size organization, not because of what we had done but what we were capable of doing.

When we got the deal, we stepped back and asked ourselves what companies like Volvo were starved for which they did not get from large service providers. This questioning led to a critical positioning exercise. We narrowed the reasons down to three: access, attention and agility. Large organizations engaging a global software partner require accessibility (not at a CEO to CEO level, but at the level of operating people); attention to what may be their business-critical and time-sensitive needs in times of complexity; and finally agility to rapidly create custom solutions to stay ahead of competition.

We took the message of access, attention and agility to many companies, such as AIG, the largest insurance firm in the US, and won their business. Down the line, we discovered that just as large customers looked for access, attention and agility, high performance individuals needed the very same attributes; working for big companies that were like anthills, they missed the intimacy and shared vision. To them, MindTree made more sense.

During the prolonged downturn, MindTree's R&D services business did not lose faith. The research work in short-range wireless went on. We started licensing our Bluetooth protocol stack technology to companies like Sony in Japan, Cherry in Europe and Silicon Wave in the US (which later became part of Qualcomm). After two years of hibernation, the market started opening up and we began hiring again. Our investments in process development, knowledge management and people practices started getting noticed and MindTree attracted many good people from leading engineering and management campuses as well as from larger competitors. We started appearing in industry surveys on best employers in India. Thanks to our frugal management style, we became cash positive after 2002 and despite the difficult times managed to become profitable in each of the following years.

It looked like the gloom was finally receding.

CHAPTER 22

Building Emotional Infrastructure

In the spring of 2004, Ashok asked me to return to India. Everyone was coming to terms with the fact that nothing was going to be the same ever again, and life had to move on. At MindTree, we were back on a rapid growth trajectory. That rapid growth had to be managed carefully because, as Peter Drucker has said, all growth can be inherently destructive. Growth brings with itself a struggle between the centrifugal forces that want to explore the boundaries of limit and the centripetal forces that want to hold on to what is the core. Unless the two are in harmony, there is the inevitability of an organization caving in under its own ambitions. The following summer, Susmita and I wound up our establishment, said goodbye to our two daughters who were now studying at Rutgers University and headed back to Bangalore one more time.

In March 2006, MindTree crossed the magical hundred million dollar mark. In the process, we became the first Indian IT services company to achieve this in all of six years. We had also completed the first phase of a new campus off the Mysore Road in Bangalore and work had commenced on the next phase. In parallel, we had decided that we would build a large campus in Chennai. We started looking at Bhubaneswar as a possible third location and talks were in progress with the government there. Under the business leadership of KK and Jani, several new customers were pouring in. Scott was now looking after the US, Anjan had moved to London to look after Europe; we were well rooted in the Middle East, in Asia and the Far East including Japan. MindTree's revenue stream was predictable enough and now we focussed on restructuring the company along industry lines so that, in addition to solid delivery capability, we could build domain knowledge. In certain areas in which we did not have capability to build from within, we started picking leaders from the industry who could build strong businesses for us. MindTree's unique culture helped us attract several senior people from various leading organizations and gave them the space to become start-ups within a start-up.

¤

I believe that organization building is akin to the creation of infrastructure. The rule of infrastructure is very simple. To be able to use it, you must first build it. It must be built ahead of its need. Think of it this way: You have to build a house before you can live in it. You cannot cross a bridge unless you have built it. The job of every leader is to continuously build infrastructure.

Leaders need to view infrastructure at three levels: the physical, the intellectual and the emotional.

The first is the easiest to comprehend and create. Put money on the ground and you will have it. But, it is also the easiest to mimic.

Intellectual infrastructure on the other hand does not come just because you have money in your pocket. It needs thought leadership and engagement. It consists of your systems, processes, methodologies and assets like intellectual property in the form of trademarks, patents, copyrights, etc. The intellectual infrastructure of an organization creates differentiation. But even that differentiation can be fleeting.

What makes a corporation truly memorable and provides it with not just differentiation but defence is its emotional infrastructure. Emotional infrastructure is a collection of all the emotional assets of an organization; it is the shared consciousness and the soul of the enterprise. It goes beyond just culture.

Building emotional infrastructure is the most difficult management challenge. It takes the longest and becomes the source of the most formidable competitive advantage. In raising MindTree, we saw our task as a simultaneous effort to build all the three forms of infrastructure. During this process, we realized that there are eight key parts to building emotional infrastructure. These are:

leadership proximity, unique rituals that communicate the idea of the organization from one group to another, rich communication, alternative support networks for people, bonding through adversity, vision, values and building a sense of exclusivity. Later, I worked with Professor Vijay Govindarajan of Tuck School in externalizing this framework and testing it in other successful organizations. Among the eight, the most difficult to build is values.

As MindTree grew in size, we faced quite a few challenges in building a shared understanding of the values we stood for. New people who came on board sometimes brought a lax attitude towards integrity, for example. Despite Ashok personally speaking to each new MindTree Mind on CLASS (Caring, Learning, Achieving, Sharing and Social Responsibility), we found that there was inadequate internalization. In an industry overheated with job opportunities, it was becoming increasingly common to fake resumés or overstate past earnings in order to land a better pay packet. At one stage, we had to terminate the services of eighty people in a single year for tampering with their past employment information. We decided to take the issue head on. We published a company document called 'All About Integrity' where we openly talked about instances of value transgression and our low tolerance on such issues. We made it available as a book to the public at large. The story of our governance standards reached the outside world and it discouraged the inflow of undesirable talent into the organization.

In the years between 2004 and 2007, we were able to establish a superior position in the minds of our prospects and our customers by delivering many mission-critical applications, unlike many larger and some formidable competitors. Less than one per cent of our business came from staff augmentation. We remained true to our original purpose of creating high-end applications for our customers. In the process, we created optimization algorithms that improved turnaround time for ships berthing in the busiest ports. We designed dealer management systems for global automotive manufacturers. Our applications ran complex reservation systems on which billion dollar businesses rested. We architected and designed large data warehouses; we mined and analysed terabytes of retail data for global customers so that multinational companies could take smarter decisions. On the R&D side, we created embedded applications that went into energy saving, into surveillance and control systems and every conceivable appliance. Our technology lit up airport runways, assisted in aerial reconnaissance over the Amazon, helped in emission control and blocked network debilitating computer viruses.

While many companies build great technical products, few understand the importance of knowledge management. As a young company, our systems and processes around knowledge management were carefully designed so that we could build human capital along with structural and customer capital. Our efforts brought us huge business value and at the same time great peer recognition by inclusion in MAKE.

We felt the time was right for MindTree to enter the capital market and be listed. After six months of careful preparation, we applied to be simultaneously listed on the Bombay Stock Exchange and the National Stock Exchange. In the following weeks, the market started sliding and became soft. Many wondered if this was indeed a good time to raise money! But to us, it did not matter. We divided amongst ourselves the global financial markets for roadshows. After a kick-off in Mumbai, Ashok and KK went to Singapore and Hong Kong. Jani, Rostow and I went to New York, Boston, London, Paris and Frankfurt. Parthasarathy, Kalyan Banerjee and Vinod Deshmukh went to all the financial centres in India. We informed the investor world that MindTree was now ready to become the first venture-funded IT services company emerging out of India to become listed on a stock exchange. The MindTree story had already reached the financial world. Wherever we went, people had heard of MindTree's management depth, culture, values, high quality of work and our people practices. Despite a sluggish market, when the IPO opened on 14 February 2007 the issue was oversubscribed a staggering 103 times. While we had sought to raise all of fifty-four million dollars in additional equity, 5.6 billion dollars poured in from investors from all over the world.

¤

Many people thought that our lives would change drastically after the IPO. Questions were raised about the level of interest the founders would have in continuing to work for the company and give their best for the next phase of the organizational journey. Questions were also raised about the company's ability to withstand the pressure of being a listed company. In reality, nothing much changed. For one thing, Ashok himself was clear that he would continue to work full-time till he was seventy and that was a good six years away. KK, Jani and I were going to turn fifty in the same year and the average age of the next level of leaders was below forty-five. Over the years, we had built up a great second and third line of leadership. We were already running MindTree with the discipline, accountability and governance systems of a listed company.

The leadership team signed off on a broad vision of the future—to build a billion dollar enterprise that would be strongly consulting led, focussed on creation of intellectual property and be globally admired for people practices. And that meant starting all over again.

Most companies that were born along with MindTree did not exist any more. At MindTree, eight years on, from start-up to its public listing, all the ten founders remained, a cohesion that is globally rare. The ten of us came from three different nationalities, two continents and three different professional backgrounds. What united us was an aspiration to build something memorable and be bound together by strong professional values and unimpeachable personal integrity. The team attracted like minded but often more competent people to come on board as time went by.

CHAPTER 23

Servant Leadership

In Koraput, we used to live in an awkwardly designed, isolated government house with no electricity or water. The redeeming feature of that house was large spaces outside that belonged to no one. There, in the long afternoons, after lunch, my mother and I would dig the obstinate earth with her kitchen utensils. The first year we planted a few saplings, white ants ate them all. Then we took ash from the embers and mixed it with the soil and dug again. The mountainous land exploded in a riot of colour as if it had been waiting for aeons for someone to come and help it bloom. As her little assistant, I watched my mother grow her roses and dahlias, zinnias and petunias. After a season was over, we carefully stored the seeds for the next year to plant them afresh.

Inside the house was a large courtyard where she and I grew beans, gourds and chilli. She always told me that I had green fingers.

On one side of the veranda was a large, bare room where she slept on the floor with my brother and me. At the far end of the room, she kept her trunk that had no lock—I periodically inspected it hoping to find something I could use but there wasn't anything useful for me. It contained the sari she had worn at her wedding, a couple of more austere cotton saris with red borders, a blouse or two, all neatly kept with naphthalene balls to prevent moths. Though I found nothing useful there, I just loved the smell each time I opened it.

My father used to sleep in a bare room on the floor, next to our room. On a wooden bracket would hang two pairs of trousers and shirts. On the wall, there was a calendar of Krishna playing the flute. He stood in silence in front of it for a few seconds, eyes closed, after coming back from work every day. But for that one photograph, he was non-denominational in his beliefs. I never saw him visit a temple or take interest in mother's religious rituals. But he believed in the teachings of Krishna in the Bhagavad Gita. When he died, all he left behind were two pocket-book editions of the great epic which I inherited. Every morning, while the night sky was still to light up, aware that the darkness would soon lift, I would awaken to the singing of an enchanting devotional song, coming from father's room. He was no great singer, but I did not know that. My groggy awareness would fill up with his voice:

Maine chakar rakho ji . . .
Chakar rahasun, bag lagasun
Niti teri darshan paasun
Vrindavan ki kunj galin mein
Tere lila gasun
Maine chakar rakho ji . . .

O, Lord make me your servant,
As your servant, I will tend to the gardens in the
    charmed bylanes of Vrindavan
and there, O Lord, I will get to see you every day
and there I will sing your praise.

Father's singing was the signal for the household to awaken, for mother to go to the courtyard and wash her face from a bucket of water kept overnight below the starlit sky, and then go and light the hearth for the family's morning cup of tea.

¤

On 31 May 2007, I turned fifty years old. I took the day off and spent time with Susmita in a quiet, reflective mood. A deep sense of fulfilment pervaded. In the silence of our togetherness, I began to hear the little drummer in me. First the beats were barely audible, like a faint whisper coming through the mist of a dark winter night. Then it began to get louder and nearer. I recognized the beat: I had heard it many times in my life. It signalled a cross-over; every time it brought a new beginning.

The next day, I spoke to Ashok and conveyed that I

would like to step down from a position of authority in MindTree to take on a position of service.

'What will you call yourself?' he asked.

I heard myself say, 'Gardener.'

'That is a good thought. Write down the role description,' he replied.

As we braced to face the challenges of taking MindTree to the next level, I clearly saw the need to develop two kinds of management roles. Some had to be structural roles and some had to break the traditional mould and work without a formal structure. I saw my task cut out for me in the second role; I wanted to focus on creating leadership capacity with the top hundred people at MindTree. I wanted to work at the grassroots level with MindTree's forty-five communities of practice that are voluntary groups fostering innovation. They serve as a powerful support network for our people. Working with senior leaders at a personal level and with these voluntary groups required freedom from a traditional corporate structure and I was now ready for a life of servant leadership. We agreed that effective 1 April 2008, MindTree would have its first Gardener. As T.S. Eliot wrote in *The Four Quartets*:

> We shall not cease from exploration
> And the end of all our exploring
> Will be to arrive where we started
> And know the place for the first time . . .

CHAPTER 24

Life's Personal Angels

From Patnagarh to the public listing of MindTree, my life has been filled with learning by observing, learning by doing and continuously learning how to learn. Amidst it all, sometimes a key lesson has been delivered to me in a mysterious manner. An unusual individual, a personal angel, has come to tell it in the passing—a few words of wisdom, an allegorical narrative, an incident from their own lives. In *The Alchemist* Paulo Coelho tells us when the message arrives it is difficult to understand the context, far less its true meaning. As we sharpen our ability to receive, the messages become meaningful.

I distinctly remember the day in January 1975 when we were returning home from Delhi after the Republic

Day parade. The hectic parleys had come to an end: the announcement, the briefing on protocol before meeting the prime minister, the introduction to the President of India, the press interviews were now behind me, like a dream. It was finally time to go home. I was sitting in a train. As it was getting ready to pull out of Old Delhi Railway Station, a familiar face appeared, frantically pushing through the crowd. It was the same officer who had chaired the selection panel to choose the Best Cadet of India, the same man who had asked me if I had heard about Diego Garcia. I wanted to get down but the train was about to leave. He held my hand through the window and just said, 'Son, never join the army, never join the navy and never join the air force.' The train started moving, our hands slid out of each other's clasp. That was the last time I ever met or heard from him. He was not being unpatriotic; he was simply telling me what I was not cut out for and could very well have gravitated towards. As a paratrooper and a Best Cadet of the NCC, my place was pretty much reserved at the Indian Military Academy, and had I not ruled that option out, my life would have been quite different.

¤

In 1996, I attended a training session on Six Sigma Quality at the Motorola University in Chicago. On completion of the training, on my way to the airport, I shared the ride with a colonel from the US Army. We spoke about our families. Like me, she had two young children and being parents our conversation veered towards the challenges of parenting. She made a statement that has remained with me ever since. All that good parents can do is inculcate in their children the sense that *when they make a choice, they also choose the consequences.*

Our lives are all about the choices we make and the consequences of those choices. Other than the fact that our coming into this world is not a matter of personal choice, most of life's subsequent turns are consequences of the choices we make. When we make a choice, we must know that each choice entails a set of consequences and we cannot wish away that responsibility. It is a paradigm that applies to each one of us. We live it in our daily lives and many of the conflicts that come up in our personal and professional lives emanate from our lack of willingness to admit that the consequences of our choices are indeed our own responsibility.

Many people make random job shifts and land up in the wrong roles, working for the wrong bosses or companies. People do not hesitate to approach someone for a favour that may be out of line, only to find out that the favour comes with strings attached. People choose friends in their early professional lives who are fun and cool but they become connectors to vices that stick with them for the rest of their lives. Or think of the many workplace indiscretions people commit that lead them to broken careers and families.

¤

Long after that meeting with my Angel of Choice, I was in Hawaii with my wife where I tried snorkelling and quite liked it; I decided to do it every day of my visit. Sifting through snorkels and flippers at a snorkelling equipment rental shop, I was quite unmindful of the old man who presided over his merchandise. After I had chosen my gear, paid for it and was about to walk away, he patted me on the back. Until then, I had not even registered his face. He was a man in his eighties. As I turned my attention to him, he said, 'Never think of retirement.' He explained that it was necessary to live a full life. 'Never think of retiring,' he repeated. 'When you get older, begin to reduce your work. Work less. But do not give up work.'

Why did he choose to deliver that message to me? At the time I was in my mid-forties and not even thinking about the possibility of stepping down any time soon. Yet, he thought I should receive this message and I did. Thanking him for the wise counsel, I put on my snorkelling equipment and went into the sea. Under the blue waters, I saw god's creation. It occurred to me that the fish, the sea urchins, the turtles, the waves, the earth, the sun and the moon—none of them ever retires. In nature, you work until it is time to say goodbye. In life, too many people look at work as a burden, some consider it a curse. If we do not work, what would we do with an able body and mind? In the IT industry, talk of retirement is a popular fib: everyone wants to earn a million, build a house, send the kids to a good school and retire. It is such a wasteful thought. All we need to do is take a walk in a busy marketplace one morning and look at the number of daily wage earners who are looking for the opportunity to work. Yet, thousands of us who do not have to deal with such uncertainty want to simply stop working! We do not realize how lucky we are to be able to get up in the morning and go some place where work awaits us.

¤

The most recent of my angels appeared in 2007. He was my landlord, who had a town house to rent us in Bridgewater, New Jersey. A thin, energetic man in his sixties, he drove a pick-up truck and had managed a forty-person consulting engineering company all his life. He had started his business a long time ago and had met a woman he loved in the course of work. They lived together for twenty-five years. Towards the end, she became very ill and weeks before she died, they got married. While the two were together, they were extremely devoted to each other and he depended on her for everything. When she died, he was so lost that he went into a prolonged state of mourning. He lost all interest in the world, not to talk about the business that both of them had built together. He would get up in the morning, have his breakfast and sleep off again. For years, he decayed. He was simply not in control of himself or his life. Then, one day, he decided to take charge and reclaim his life. He went back to work and brought his company back in shape in a year. Today, he is still lonely without her but he is healing through his work and is moving on.

During the course of telling us this very difficult story, my landlord shared a message from one of his angels. When he was studying engineering, there was a compulsory course on relationships. A Chinese professor taught him that subject. The professor told him, 'Open your mind before you open your mouth.' I was struck by the simplicity of this idea. How often in our everyday relationships, at home and at work, with friends and colleagues, are we quick to open our mouths even before we open our minds? How vastly different every dialogue, every engagement, every attempt at issue resolution would become if only we remembered this simple thought: 'Open your mind before you open your mouth.'

In the journey called life, as we are engulfed in the everyday grind, chasing our successes and trying to survive the failures, we constantly look for the golden formula. There is, in reality, no golden formula, just a set of lessons. Some are delivered to us by people whom we come in casual contact with, and as time goes by, we begin to understand that each one of us has personal angels—the people who live in our midst.

CHAPTER 25

Go Kiss the World

In the course of my professional career, I have met heads of states, CEOs of Fortune 500 companies, some great men of religion and practising leaders from many walks of life. Each one has made me think and some have left a great impression on me. I have also been deeply impacted by countless ordinary people whose life and living revolves around the here and now. Like the man who sold cucumbers on a Chennai street who left me feeling inadequate about my education and level of engagement with current issues. Or the vegetable vendor in Bangalore who had lost his day's earnings when his pushcart laden with tomatoes upturned at a busy intersection in front of my eyes who made me question my personal values in life. In search of life's lessons, I have also followed a cardiac surgeon and watched heart surgery on a new-born baby and seen a procedure being conducted by a group of neurosurgeons on a human brain. I have listened, fascinated, to software architects, builders of bridges, astronauts, dancers and actors. My entire life has also been an enchanted journey from one land to another—I have sat next to strangers in planes and trains and buses in alien lands, I have made friends with taxi drivers whom I would never meet again, have heard their life's story in the proverbial forty-five-minute ride to downtown and found familiarity and learning in them. I share here a few of the important lessons I have learnt in my life.

It's all in the mind

My most significant lesson is that everything we achieve begins in our minds. Whether it is the long march of Moses across the desert to give deliverance to his people, Mahatma's Gandhi's assertion that one day India would be a free nation, Mohamed Yunus's dream that poor village women in Bangladesh would have access to credit without collateral or Jack Welch's vision to make GE a global company—everything begins in the mind as an idea, a dream. If we believe in the idea strongly enough and are willing to give it our very best, everything is possible. It is our conviction that breathes life into an idea and makes it a living thing. The Kathopanishad tells us:

> You are your deep driving desire
> As is your desire, so is your will

As is your will, so is your act
As is your act, so is your Destiny.

The power to receive

The second lesson life has taught me is that the power to receive is far more important than the power to give. The act of receiving is far more significant in the overall scheme of things. It is an important lesson for those who give and then see that their giving has made no difference. One has to be blessed to receive. A good example is the family. Imagine parents of four children who raise them in a very comparable manner; yet the four children may grow up to be very different people in their own lives. One may become rich and successful and insular, one poor but willing to help, another leads a life of principles and another develops a flexible moral code and blames it on the environment. The input from the two parents remaining the same, the output can be so vastly different. The power is then not in the giving; it is in the extended hand that receives. What matters is the capability to catalyse what you have received.

To get, you must first give

Marc Andreessen, the man behind Netscape Navigator, gave away copies of his software free to the world while it was in its beta state. This was counter-intuitive in a world that is obsessed with copyrights. Here was a potentially world-beating concept, and he was giving it away free. No one at that time, not even Microsoft, knew about the impending commercial power of the Internet, not to talk about the browser. The result of giving away Netscape Navigator was that thousands of early adopters gratefully used it, found bugs and areas for improvement and reported back to Andreessen. As a result, he had an army of software wizards all over the world who were working on his product for him for free! People who give are people who get. We need to develop an expansive view of life; we need to believe that there is more in it for everyone if everyone is involved and benefits. Leaders must develop a mindset of abundance, not scarcity, as they build their organizational vision.

Connect with people

In the corporate environment, I have come across scores of brilliant people who have great grades in engineering and management. But as many of these people work their way up their careers, they do not make it to the top. Something crucial is missing. They never connect with people. They often fail to grasp critical situations or fail to take charge when a boat is leaking. Sometimes, they lack common sense. I came to realize that many such people, despite their high Intelligence Quotient (IQ), are emotionally inept: they do not build empathy with people around them. Daniel Goleman tells us that unlike IQ, which we all come factory-fitted with and cannot change, in life we can evolve our Emotional Quotient (EQ) and with it become more effective in our day-to-day dealings. As human beings, we *feel* even before we think. People who connect with us at the level of our feelings build memorable association. It is our empathy that helps us connect with the world. When a leader connects at the level of feelings, he can get his people to aspire to dizzying heights and create in them the will and ability to scale them.

Life is constant negotiation

As you look around, you will find that in life everything is possible. There is enough evidence of that fact. While this is true, at a personal level I have also learnt that in life everything is negotiable. Life throws the proverbial curve ball at us as we grow up and we begin to realize that nothing is a given, there is no such thing as a status quo. This extends itself to agreements and understandings that we reach with partners, customers, suppliers, parents, siblings, our own children, and spouse. Situations can change overnight. Such is the dynamic nature of the world that we need to face an emergent situation with an even temperament and look for the most beneficial outcome for all concerned, given the new set of circumstances. Leaders must look at things as they are, not as we wish they should have been. While a leader's job is to alter the reality, he cannot begin by looking at life with an altered reality.

The slippery slope of overachievement

I have dealt with many overachievers in my life. I believe that I have a high achievement orientation myself. Because the subject of high achievement is of great personal interest to me, I have watched myself like a shadow, and I have come to realize that overachievement comes with a price tag. If not handled well, there is a danger that things will spin out of control at the very height of your professional career for reasons that often beat common sense. Many examples abound, from Bill Clinton's legendary indiscretion to professionals at work who do strange things that destroy their reputations and years of good work in a single, stupid move. Many overachievers create their own perception of reality and develop resultant problems in dealing with other people. When I see such people struggle with situations, I tell myself that sometimes one has to be blessed to be ordinary. The capacity to overachieve needs to be seen as a gift from above, something we simply hold in trust, a capacity that has been given to us to create larger benefit for others; it is something that can be taken away at a moment's notice. Viewing it in this sense creates humility, which is essential when fighting the sense of altered reality most overachievers create for themselves.

One frequent theme for high achievers is frustration. High achievers set high standards for themselves and expect everyone else to follow them. This is a legitimate but sometimes unreasonable position. As a result, they tend to get easily frustrated, especially with the system. Frustration without the capability to change things is like a radioactive material burning inside you. Your frustration is the difference between your ambition and your capability. Either improve your capability or lower your ambition. Do not just sit there with the radioactivity turned inward.

Not everything around you can be changed by you. The world's job is not to follow you just because *you* have figured things out before others. You should only be pained to change things that you can take charge of and create a sustainable impact. This is where Steven Covey's concept of zone of concern and zone of influence comes in. Focus on those issues that fall in the overlap of your zone of concern and zone of influence. Concern without influence is of no use.

The marginal person is important

In my life, I have understood that trying to please your boss is not beneficial in the long run. For the boss who expects you to curry favour, no gift is big enough; he will always think of it as his entitlement. On the other hand, if you are considerate towards your juniors, those below you, greet them with a pat, a smile or a nice word, you will be remembered for a lifetime. In exchange, they will walk to the end of the world for you. So, do not waste your time trying to please the big bosses. Focus on the little people. In a harshly competitive world, that may sound counter-intuitive. But believe me, when you focus on the small folk, you create a constituency that no boss can ever ignore.

Passion is what passion does

My next lesson has to do with some overpassionate

people. At MindTree's Bangalore office, a bright young lady joined us from a leading multinational organization from the US. She had passionate views on everything around her—from leadership issues to women's empowerment to innovation to how to improve the smallest thing in administration. Her thoughts were incisive; she always knew what was wrong and what needed to be done. After a particular incident of sexual harassment in the organization, I had invited Linda Howard, an international authority on the subject, to talk to our people. Linda's work with us brought out a few related issues and one of the things we realized was the need to create a women's council within the organization. However, that needed to be a grassroots organization, to be run with voluntary power. The passionate young lady put together a vision and value document and asked for a meeting with me. We sat down to discuss in great detail what could be achieved by the proposed council. I was very impressed with the draft charter. To me it was lofty and difficult, hence worthwhile. Such a charter would require a long view of time and tremendous servant leadership. At the end of her presentation, I told her that she should undertake it only if she was willing to give the idea at least three years of her own time. She froze at my suggestion. Then, somewhat uncomfortably, she said that she had already put in her papers and was going back to her earlier organization because they had made her an offer she just could not refuse. I was not disappointed with her decision to leave; I was disappointed with her passion. Passion to me is what passion does. Too many people know what is wrong with the world. Their knowledge and intensity do not matter. What matters is making a small but real difference. That is why the Mahatma said, 'Be the change you want to see.'

The power of resilience

Another very important lesson in my life is about tenacity. When you look around and see great people in positions of organizational leadership and then compare them with their juniors, you find the latter can often be more brilliant, more competent and more intelligent. But the leader outshines them in his resilience. Sometimes, it is not inherent competence but one's resilience that decides who the winner is, particularly in the long run. As a marathon runner knows, success is about your capability to withstand pain, longer. In business and in life, you come across numerous instances when you feel that all the odds are stacked against you, life is truly coming to an end; the prophets of gloom will provide you convincing data on why you should leave and never come back. In times like this, just hang in there.

The key to happiness is not money

Billionaire Warren Buffet, one of the richest men in the world, is reported to have said that any amount in excess of ten thousand dollars does not bring 'happiness'. The implicit message is simple—you can acquire any amount of material success you want, but do not expect *that* to be the source of your happiness. This does not mean you should give up the desire to earn, but in doing so, keep low expectations on its ability to give you happiness. Remember the day in your life when you received a hefty and unexpected pay rise? How long did that pleasurable feeling last? What happened after that? Money is important in life but not the source of any lasting happiness.

Look beyond yourself

A children's ward in a hospital is a great place for life's lessons. Susmita and I were very young when Neha, our first child, was born. When she was barely six months' old, she suffered from acute broncholitis and had serious trouble breathing. Neha was hospitalized and lay asleep under an oxygen tent. I was devastated because she was my little baby; I wished I could breathe for her. I knew how much she was suffering because as a child I had suffered with asthma. I wanted the whole world to attend to her and the hospital staff to hover around her. I was feeling extremely anxious and lonely and desperate. Then I realized that right there in the same room was a ten-year-old boy who was undergoing dialysis. He had no attendants. Later I learnt his poor family was worn out by his ordeal, so the boy was there all by himself, left in the care of the hospital and god. In the two days that Neha stayed in the hospital, I saw many such children, each fighting his or her own battle, some remarkably cheerfully, and learnt that my pain is only as large as my inability to see pain elsewhere.

Real men say sorry

As we grow up, from time to time we make mistakes. Sometimes, we hurt people's feelings. In most instances, the hurt caused is unintended. But, nonetheless, for the person who feels the pain, it is real. Once we realize we have hurt someone, we spend an enormous amount of time explaining rationally why the other person should not have felt that way. This is unnecessary; the only reason we get into all that explanation is our ego. The moment calls for just three words: 'I am sorry.' Great leaders are people who can quickly and genuinely say that they are sorry. By saying sorry, you do not become weak. You shorten the path from the head to the heart.

Learn to forgive yourself

From time to time, I meet many outstanding leaders who, somewhere in the recesses of their minds, hold a grudge against a loved one, a mentor or some other person who might have fallen from grace many years ago. It affects them in a deeply personal manner and surfaces from time to time. In life, one must learn to forgive others and, sometimes, forgive oneself.

Self-doubt is positive

My final lesson for you is about self-doubt. Periodically,

we are all entitled to self-doubt. There will be moments when you feel you are at a crossroads; times when you question the very meaning of life and the existence of god. You are not the only one to feel this way. It is a rite of passage. People who create great impact suffer from moments of great soul-searching. In itself, it is a good sign because from the depth of our self-doubt we learn to let go; from that emerges a conviction and with it comes the capability to go kiss the world.

 Epilogue

After my first book *The High-Performance Entrepreneur* was published to reader acclaim, I wondered what else I could give my readers. In 2004, I delivered the inaugural speech to the Class of 2004 at the Indian Institute of Management, Bangalore, titled 'Go, Kiss the World'. In that I spoke about my upbringing in small-town India, how my parents raised me, and I shared the lessons I had learnt from my parents. I had no idea that the speech would develop a life of its own over the Internet. I was overwhelmed with the response it generated and it occurred to me that I could share my entire life with my readers and, wrapped around it, a few lessons from my personal journey of hope.

Reading about my parents and my childhood, you may feel that I have had to struggle in my early life. It never really felt that way. I want to clarify that I did not *struggle* during my childhood. It was a life of simplicity, not struggle. My story is not one of overcoming deprivation and poverty. My life is about contentment, about the possibility that ordinary people can aim to do extraordinary things. I am proud of the material simplicity my parents had and have never felt deprived. My childhood was rich with a sense of continuous wonder, affection and learning. I hope I have been able to impart this through my words.

The purpose of writing this book is to tell millions of young professionals and particularly people in small-town India that it is possible to make it in life, like I did. But *making it* in life is not about material benefits and carving individual success; it is about moving from brightness to greater brightness, while taking people along. It is not about making it big, but about making it good.

Further Reading

If you like my book, you may like to read the following:

1. *Jonathan Livingston Seagull* by Richard Bach.
2. *Future Shock* by Alvin Toffler.
3. *What They Do Not Teach You at Harvard Business School* by Mark McCormack.
4. *Emotional Intelligence* by Daniel Goleman.
5. *Working with Emotional Intelligence* by Daniel Goleman.
6. *Social Intelligence* by Daniel Goleman.
7. *The Road Less Traveled* by Scott Peck.
8. *The Soul of a New Machine* by Tracy Kidder.
9. *Long Walk to Freedom* by Nelson Mandela.
10. *Freedom at Midnight* by Larry Collins and Dominique Lapierre.
11. *Gandhi* by Louis Fischer.
12. *The Attention Economy* by Thomas Davenport.

13. *Paraja* by Gopinath Mohanty, translated into English by Bikram K. Das.

14. *The Alchemist* by Paulo Coelho.

15. *The Meme Machine* by Susan Blackmore.

16. *The Fifth Discipline* by Peter Senge.

17. *It's Not About the Bike: My Journey Back to Life* by Lance Armstrong.

18. *India: A Wounded Civilization* by V.S. Naipaul.

19. *Management Challenges for the 21st Century* by Peter Drucker.

20. *The Four Quartets* by T.S. Eliot.

21. *Theory U* by Otto Scharmer.

22. *Presence* by Peter Senge, Otto Scharmer, Jospeh Jarowski and Betty SueFlowers.

23. *Five Minds for the Future* by Howard Gardner.

The High-Performance Entrepreneur

Golden Rules for Success in Today's World

Subroto Bagchi

'Highly readable, crisply written...inspirational reading for any new Indian entrepreneur'—*Frontline*

Difficult though setting up a business is, becoming a high-performance entrepreneur is harder still. And yet, of the many thousands who try, there are those who go on to become successful; some even graduate to setting up companies that hold their own against the toughest competition, becoming icons of achievement. In *The High-Performance Entrepreneur*, Subroto Bagchi draws upon his own highly successful experience to offer guidance from the idea stage to the IPO level. More than just a guide, this is a book that will tap the entrepreneurial energy within you.

We Are Like That Only

Understanding the Logic of Consumer India

Rama Bijapurkar

With a billion plus consumers India is one of the largest, most varied and stratified markets in the world today. It is young, with rising incomes and purchasing power, and has only just begun its consumption journey. Every marketer would want a piece of what may arguably be the largest untapped market in the world.

Irreverent and insightful, this book casts an unblinking eye on twelve key facets of Consumer India. It successfully fathoms how much Indians earn, how they consume, what they consume and what dictates their consumption choices. A powerful book, it is the definitive epitaph for formula strategy approaches to India's consumer markets, especially of the 'global' transplant kind.

What the Customer Wants You to Know

How Everybody Needs to Think
Differently About Sales

Ram Charan

From the bestselling author of *What the CEO Wants You to Know*--how to rethink sales from the outside in.

More than ever these days, the sales process often turns into a war about price—a frustrating, unpleasant war that takes all the fun out of selling. But there's a better way to think about sales, says bestselling author Ram Charan, who is famous for clarifying and simplifying difficult business problems.

Someday, every company will listen more closely to the customer, and every manager will realize that sales is everyone's business, not just the sales department's. In the meantime, this eye-opening book will show you how to get started.

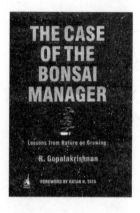

The Case of the Bonsai Manager

Lessons from Nature on Growing

R. Gopalakrishnan

No one sets out to become a bonsai manager, just as no plant is created by Nature to be a bonsai. Managers' growth can be stunted by their own acts of omission and commission—instead, they should branch out in new directions drawing on their innate genius.

Drawing on insights from a rich management career spanning forty years, this book gives an idea of the basic characteristics of human nature, the complexities of employee behaviour within organizations and how an agenda for change can be charted out. This is essential because future managers will face vastly different challenges as the world around them changes dramatically. In this world, the inclusive, intuitive and humane style of management will work, not the top-down approach—and here is an author uniquely placed to tell us how.